Jacob and Esau

Birthright and Blessing

D1568875

Rev. Wallace H. Heflin

The
McDougal
Publishing
Company

All Scripture quotations are from the Authorized King
James Version of the Bible.

PUBLISHED BY:

The McDougal Publishing Company
P.O. Box 3595
Hagerstown, MD 21742-3595

ISBN 1-884369-01-4

Printed in the United States of America
For Worldwide Distribution

Dedication

I want to dedicate this book to my mother, Rev. Edith Ward Heflin, for all the years she prayed faithfully for me while I ran from my birthright. She never gave up, until I claimed what was rightfully mine.

And Isaac intreated the Lord for his wife, because she was barren: and the Lord was intreated of him, and Rebekah his wife conceived. And the children struggled together within her; and she said, If it be so, why am I thus? And she went to inquire of the Lord. And the Lord said unto her, Two nations are in thy womb, and two manner of people shall be separated from thy bowels; and the one people shall be stronger than the other people; and the elder shall serve the younger.

And when her days to be delivered were fulfilled, behold, there were twins in her womb. And the first came out red, all over like an hairy garment; and they called his name Esau. And after that came his brother out, and his hand took hold on Esau's heel; and his name was called Jacob: and Isaac was threescore years old when she bare them.

And the boys grew: and Esau was a cunning hunter, a man of the field; and Jacob was a plain man, dwelling in tents. And Isaac loved Esau, because he did eat of his venison: but Rebekah loved Jacob. And Jacob sod pottage: and Esau came from the field, and he was faint: And Esau said to Jacob, Feed me, I pray thee, with that same red pottage; for I am faint: therefore was his name called Edom. And Jacob said, Sell me this day thy birthright. And Esau said, Behold, I am at the point to die: and what profit shall this birthright do to me? And Jacob said, Swear to me this day; and he sware unto him: and he sold his birthright unto Jacob. Then Jacob gave Esau bread and pottage of lentiles; and he did eat and drink, and rose up, and went his way: thus Esau despised his birthright.   Genesis 25:21-34

Contents

Introduction

Introduction

Birthright and blessing: what do those two words mean? Are they the same? Are they different? Does the birthright still exist in New Testament times? Is the blessing for us today?

This book is the result of a revelation that God gave me late one night, many years ago, in which He showed me that the traditional teaching on this subject is not only wrong but dangerous. Through the years, my search for more understanding of the birthright and the blessing, which I discovered that night to be two distinct promises, has led me into new areas of truth. Because these discoveries have challenged and enlightened my own personal life and enriched my own ministry, I have shared them with God's people all over the world in preachings and teachings. Now, for the first time, I am happy to be able to share them with God's people everywhere in printed form.

Perhaps even more valuable to me than the lessons of the birthright and blessing, have been the lessons I have learned from the Bible account of the differences between the brothers, Esau and Jacob. These lessons have consistently contributed to the further development of my own spiritual potential and to those with whom I have been privileged to share their secrets.

Open your heart as you read *Jacob and Esau: Birthright and Blessing,* and allow the God of Abraham, Isaac and Jacob to bless you richly. He is ready to do it, if you are ready to receive His blessing.

Rev. Wallace H. Heflin
Ashland, Virginia

Part I

A Recipe for Disaster

There is, in this life, a great division between the light and the darkness. A mighty battle is waged in every man's life between the flesh and the spirit. So intense is this struggle of human kind that even in mighty and strong Christians, the effect is felt. St. Paul said:

> *For that which I do I allow not: for what I would, that do I not; but what I hate, that do I.*
> *But I see another law in my members, warring against the law of my mind, and bringing me into captivity to the law of sin which is in my members.*
> Romans 7:15 & 23

Nowhere in Scripture is this amazing saga recorded in such poignancy as in the story of Jacob and Esau, the twin sons of Isaac and Rebekah. Spiritual Jacob struggled against carnal Esau even in their mother's womb and the forces at work within her perplexed Rebekah and caused her to inquire about it of God.

During this struggle, enmity was unleashed that would influence world history for a thousand generations. As the children were being born into the world, spiritual Jacob reached out to pull Esau back from his coveted firstborn status and privileges by grasping him by the heel, attempting to prevent him from attaining the preeminence. Thus began a lifelong struggle between flesh and spirit.

Chapter 1

Children of a Miracle

And Isaac intreated the Lord for his wife, because she was barren: and the Lord was intreated of him, and Rebekah his wife conceived.   Genesis 25:21

There are six other miraculous births recorded in the Bible. Interestingly enough, they run in pairs whose names begin with the same letter. They are Samuel and Samson, Jesus and John (the Baptist), Ishmael and Isaac. Jesus' birth was different from the others, in that He experienced an immaculate conception. He was conceived by the Holy Ghost, while the other five had natural fathers.

Abraham and Sarah, who were destined to become the progenitors of the Jewish race, needed a miracle.

They had no heir yet, and they were growing old. Twenty-four years had passed since God had given them the promise of this blessing. Abraham had been seventy-five when God spoke to him, and now he was only a few years away from being 100. Time was quickly running out for them. Only the Word of the Lord could perform such a miracle, because Sarah was well past the childbearing age.

> *Now Abraham and Sarah were old and well stricken in age; and it ceased to be with Sarah after the manner of women.*   Genesis 18:11

But it happened. Isaac was born when Abraham was already one hundred years old. God will do whatever is needed to bring His Word to pass.

Isaac and Rebekah found themselves in need of a similar miracle. After twenty years of life together, they had still not produced any offspring. Rebekah was barren, as had been Sarah. Isaac had been forty years old when they married, so he was now sixty and was not getting any younger. At this point Isaac became concerned and began talking to God about the matter. Remembering the example of his parents and the miracle of his own birth, he knew what God could do. Needless to say, God heard Isaac's prayer and caused Rebekah to miraculously conceive.

The Struggle Within Rebekah's Womb

> *And the children struggled together within her; and she said, If it be so, why am I thus? And she went to inquire of the Lord. And the Lord said*

unto her, Two nations are in thy womb, and two manner of people shall be separated from thy bowels; and the one people shall be stronger than the other people; and the elder shall serve the younger.
Genesis 25:22-23

Rebekah's pregnancy was not an easy one. It was so difficult, in fact, that she asked the Lord why. Normally, women of that day went to a Hebrew midwife to share their difficulties and ask advice. But Rebekah went to God instead. That was the right thing to do. God has the answer we are looking for. As men, we are limited by our intellect and experience, but God is not limited. He knows everything and understands everything. He can, therefore, do what no man can do, and He can help us when no one else can. When you have a need, go to Jesus, and He will give you the answer you are looking for.

Psychologists don't have the answer. One psychiatrist told me frankly that the majority of the cases she deals with are the result of sin. I believe it. Sin is a festering sore, a deadly cancer. It will destroy you — morally, physically and emotionally. And only God has the answer for sin. Go to God.

Some will ask if I literally mean to go to God with *every* problem. Believe me, I mean just that. He is a specialist in every field, and nothing is too hard for Him. Yes, go to God about everything.

Some people pray to saints, because they consider that Jesus is too busy to answer individual prayers. Let me tell you that it is not true. He is never too busy to hear your cry, and when you need Him, He will always be there.

No problem is too insignificant for His attention. When you lose your keys, you can say, "Jesus, where are my keys?" And He will help you find them.

The Scriptures teach us to look to Jesus.

> *Looking unto Jesus the author and finisher of our faith; who for the joy that was set before him endured the cross, despising the shame, and is set down at the right hand of the throne of God.*
> Hebrews 12:2

He is not only *"the author"* of our faith. He is also *"the finisher."* He wants to keep right on blessing you and loading you with benefits. Your cry for help is not a bother to Him. He is just waiting to intercede on your behalf. He is just waiting for you to say, "Jesus, I don't know what to do. Help me." When you cry to Him in this way, He will manifest His power on your behalf and share with you His knowledge so that you can know exactly what to do in any given situation.

The main reason, I believe, that Rebekah talked to God instead of the midwife, was because she sensed that something unusual was taking place in her womb. She sensed that the discomfort she was experiencing had a spiritual cause. And she was right.

When she asked the Lord what it was she was feeling, He told her that a struggle was taking place in her womb, that she was carrying two children, twin sons, and that two groups of very different people would come forth from those two sons. And, surprisingly, He said that the older would serve the younger.

Who would have imagined that a woman who was barren for twenty years would give birth to twins? But that is what God said, and that is exactly what happened.

When God said that the elder would serve the younger, he was not displaying favoritism. The boys had not even been born yet. He was simply telling the facts, advising Rebekah what would actually take place.

A Jewish tradition, told to me by one of my Rabbi friends, says:

> When Rebekah passed a place of earthly prominence, a place of secular importance, Esau struggled to get out first. But when she passed a synagogue, a place of prayer, a place of worship, Jacob struggled to get out first.

Whatever the case, a struggle was going on. Twin boys were about to be born, and their birth would affect the whole world.

The Birth of Nations

> And when her days to be delivered were fulfilled, behold, there were twins in her womb. And the first came out red, all over like an hairy garment; and they called his name Esau. And after that came his brother out, and his hand took hold on Esau's heel; and his name was called Jacob: and Isaac was threescore years old when she bare them.
>   Genesis 25:24-26

The first son to be born was said to be *"red all over, like an hairy garment."* They called him Esau. But Jacob was not far behind. He was holding on to Esau's heel. I once asked a Jewish rabbi, "How do you account for the fact that Esau was born first, and yet Jacob is looked to as the spiritual leader of Israel?" I was amazed by his answer:

"That is easy to answer" he said. "If you put two large objects into a bag, the one you put in first will come out last. Jacob was born second, but we believe that he was conceived first." What an interesting concept!

Try it. Put two cantaloupes into a bag. The cantaloupe you put in first will come out last, and the cantaloupe you put in last will come out first.

Nothing more is said in the Bible about the unusual birth of these two boys.

The Boys Grow Up

And the boys grew: and Esau was a cunning hunter, a man of the field; and Jacob was a plain man, dwelling in tents.   Genesis 25:27

I am sure that the differences in these two boys were evident from a very early age; for, when they had grown, the Bible describes them as two very different individuals. It shows Esau as a man of the outdoors, a rugged individualist who didn't like to be fenced in.

Jacob, on the other hand, is shown as more of a home body, the studious type, who loved to spend time at his mother's knee, hearing the stories of valor of God's people. The scene is set for a classic confrontation.

Chapter 2

Birthright and Blessing

And Jacob sod pottage: and Esau came from the field, and he was faint: And Esau said to Jacob, Feed me, I pray thee, with that same red pottage; for I am faint: therefore was his name called Edom. And Jacob said, Sell me this day thy birthright. And Esau said, Behold, I am at the point to die: and what profit shall this birthright do to me? And Jacob said, Swear to me this day; and he sware unto him: and he sold his birthright unto Jacob. Then Jacob gave Esau bread and pottage of

lentiles; and he did eat and drink, and rose up, and
went his way: thus Esau despised his birthright.
                                        Genesis 25:29-34

The Bible account now skips directly to the next
great event in the lives of these two brothers. It occurred one day when Esau came in from hunting in
the fields and was hungry. Jacob was evidently a good
cook and had something on the stove. Esau smelled
the food that Jacob had prepared and wanted some of
it so badly that he was willing to give up something
very valuable to get it.

It is important that we understand the chronology of
these events. Many years have now gone by, and this
passage is not talking about children. It takes time to
become *"a cunning hunter."* Most boys who are raised
on the farm learn to hunt, but they don't become cunning hunters at an early age. The fact is: when the
events in question took place, the twins were now
thirty-eight years old, no longer innocent, young boys
who didn't understand what they were doing. They
were grown men who knew the importance of their
decisions.

Jacob was just waiting for an opportunity that he
was sure would present itself at some moment. He
was very willing to serve his brother, but for a price.
He demanded that Esau sell him the birthright; and
Esau, without much thought, was willing to do it.

What was this birthright that Esau was so willing to
give up for so little?

What Is the Birthright?

There were several elements in the birthright, but they were all basically spiritual. The eldest son of the family, the firstborn, received, upon his father's death, a spiritual inheritance. One of the important elements of that inheritance was the privilege of serving as priest of the family. That meant that he was to hear from God and to know God's will for the extended family. As priest, he was responsible to God for the spiritual welfare of the family and the direction it was taking. When the family had needs, he took those needs before the Lord in prayer. Being priest of the family was a great responsibility, but it was recognized in Israel as a great honor, a privilege. And, if the priest of the family performed his service well, he would indeed be honored and respected.

The spiritual inheritance of Isaac was much more than the normal Jewish family. To him, had fallen the promises given by God to Abraham, his father:

> *Now the Lord had said unto Abram, Get thee out of thy country, and from thy kindred, and from thy father's house, unto a land that I will shew thee: And I will make of thee a great nation, and I will bless thee, and make thy name great; and thou shalt be a blessing: And I will bless them that bless thee, and curse him that curseth thee: and in thee shall all families of the earth be blessed.*
>
> Genesis 12:1-3

Neither shall thy name any more be called Abram,
but thy name shall be Abraham; for a father of
many nations have I made thee. And I will make
thee exceeding fruitful, and I will make nations of
thee, and kings shall come out of thee.

Genesis 17:5-6

Seeing that Abraham shall surely become a great
and mighty nation, and all the nations of the earth
shall be blessed in him?   Genesis 18:18
And in thy seed shall all the nations of the earth be
blessed; because thou hast obeyed my voice.

Genesis 22:18

These mighty promises had not been fulfilled in
Abraham's time. They were not only for him, as an
individual, but for his descendants, as well; and many
of them would be fulfilled at a future date. Abraham
passed them on to Isaac at his death; and Isaac, in turn,
must pass them on to his son. One day Abraham's
heirs would bless the world. That was their right. This
right should have passed to Esau.

The important element of becoming the earth blesser
was to be the progenitor of the Messiah, the Savior of
the world, to provide *"the seed of the woman"* that
would bruise the serpent's heel.

And I will put enmity between thee and the
woman, and between thy seed and her seed; it shall
bruise thy head, and thou shalt bruise his heel.

Genesis 3:15

That godly seed which was to bruise the head of the serpent should have been of Esau's line. Instead, it came forth from Jacob, because Esau valued the privilege so little that he sold it in a moment of physical hunger. For some lentil soup and bread, he readily relinquished his right to bless all the nations of the earth.

It was lawful to sell the birthright. But it could only be sold to the next in line, as was the case with Jacob and Esau. If there had been another brother between them, Jacob could not have bought the birthright, unless it had been first offered to the next in line and had been refused. The person buying the birthright had to be willing to accept the responsibility that accompanied the birthright and be able to afford it.

So, Esau was within his rights to sell, and Jacob was within his rights to buy. Esau would later claim that Jacob had taken the birthright by deceit, but the truth is that Esau willingly sold it.

What, Then, Is the Blessing?

Many people take the birthright and the blessing to be one and the same. They are not. While the birthright was basically a spiritual inheritance, the blessing was the physical inheritance. Esau sold his birthright; then, forty years later, Jacob tried to get the blessing too — through deception. Again, it is important to understand the chronology of events. Jacob and Esau are now seventy-eight years old.

The story of how it all happened is relatively simple, but interesting.

> *And it came to pass, that when Isaac was old, and his eyes were dim, so that he could not see, he called Esau his eldest son, and said unto him, My son: and he said unto him, Behold, here am I. And he said, Behold now, I am old, I know not the day of my death: Now therefore take, I pray thee, thy weapons, thy quiver and thy bow, and go out to the field, and take me some venison; And make me savoury meat, such as I love, and bring it to me, that I may eat; that my soul may bless thee before I die.*   Genesis 27:1-4

Isaac was concerned because he was growing old. He had a right to be concerned; He was 138. His eyesight was failing, and his strength was ebbing. Sensing that his time on earth might be drawing to a close, he called Esau and told him it was time to lay hands on him, as was the custom of the patriarchs, and to pass on the blessing.

Abraham had been one of the richest men of his day.

> *And Abram was very rich in cattle, in silver, and in gold.*   Genesis 13:2

Isaac inherited the riches of his father. Now those riches were to be passed on to his sons, the greater portion, a vast fortune, going to the firstborn.

Isaac loved Esau and loved the meat Esau brought him from the hunt. He asked his son to go hunting and to bring him his favorite meat dish, venison, so that they could celebrate together one last time before he gave the blessing. Esau was eager to obey and ran to the field with his bow and arrows to hunt.

The only problem was that Rebekah overheard this conversation. She had evidently developed a habit of eavesdropping on the conversations of her hairy son and his father.

> *And Rebekah heard when Isaac spake to Esau his son. And Esau went to the field to hunt for venison, and to bring it. And Rebekah spake unto Jacob her son, saying, Behold, I heard thy father speak unto Esau thy brother, saying, Bring me venison, and make me savoury meat, that I may eat, and bless thee before the Lord before my death.*
>
> Genesis 27:5-7

Isaac considered Esau to be *"his"* son, and Rebekah considered Jacob to be *"her"* boy, so what she had overheard troubled her. She was determined that Jacob be the dominant heir, not Esau. We might forgive her, knowing that she remembered the word of the Lord, given to her before the boys were born. That word said that the younger son would be the stronger of the two and that the elder would serve the younger. But God didn't need Rebekah's help to bless Jacob. He was very capable of doing that on His own.

Rebekah was not so sure. She devised an elaborate plan, which she proceeded to tell Jacob.

Now therefore, my son, obey my voice according to that which I command thee. Go now to the flock, and fetch me from thence two good kids of the goats; and I will make them savoury meat for thy father, such as he loveth: And thou shalt bring it to thy father, that he may eat, and that he may bless thee before his death. Genesis 27:8-10

At first, Jacob didn't seem to be very keen on this idea. He was sure that his father could not be so easily fooled and wondered what would happen if they were discovered in their duplicity.

And Jacob said to Rebekah his mother, Behold, Esau my brother is a hairy man, and I am a smooth man: My father peradventure will feel me, and I shall seem to him as a deceiver; and I shall bring a curse upon me, and not a blessing.
Genesis 27:11-12

So Rebekah had to tell her son each specific step to take.

And his mother said unto him, Upon me be thy curse, my son: only obey my voice, and go fetch me them. And he went, and fetched, and brought them to his mother: and his mother made savoury

*meat, such as his father loved. And Rebekah took
goodly raiment of her eldest son Esau, which were
with her in the house, and put them upon Jacob
her younger son: And she put the skins of the kids
of the goats upon his hands, and upon the smooth
of his neck: And she gave the savoury meat and the
bread, which she had prepared, into the hand of her
son Jacob.* Genesis 27:13-17

First, he must bring her some goat's meat. She knew
how to cook it with just the right spices so that Isaac
would be fooled into believing that it was the venison
he had requested from Esau. After all, she had taught
Esau how to cook.

We consider it to be a very novel thing that we can
now buy turkey meat that tastes just like ham or ba-
con. But Rebekah knew how to do that same thing
thousands of years ago with just the right spices.

Next, Rebekah took some of the hide from the
slaughtered goats and wrapped it around Jacob's
hands and arms, knowing that if Isaac touched the
flesh of his son, it must be hairy like Esau's. She went
to the closet, where, she remembered, some of Esau's
clothes were hanging. She took some of those clothes
and told Jacob to put them on. In this way, Jacob
would have even the smell of his brother, something
very important to a person with failing sight.

With these steps taken, Jacob went quickly in to see
his father — before Esau had a chance to get home
from the hunt.

*And he came unto his father, and said, My father:
and he said, Here am I; who art thou, my son?
And Jacob said unto his father, I am Esau thy
firstborn; I have done according as thou badest me:
arise, I pray thee, sit and eat of my venison, that
thy soul may bless me. And Isaac said unto his
son, How is it that thou hast found it so quickly,
my son? And he said, Because the Lord thy God
brought it to me.*   Genesis 27:18-20

It was an ingenious plan, and, despite Jacob's reser-
vations, it worked just the way his clever mother had
planned it. But Jacob had to lie to make it work, for
when he approached Isaac, his father asked who was
coming. It was hard for him to believe that Esau was
returning so quickly from the hunt. "I am Esau, your
eldest son," Jacob assured him. "I brought the venison
you requested. Here it is. Sit up and eat, so you can
bless me."

When Isaac voiced surprise that Esau had returned
so quickly, Jacob answered, *"Your God helped me."*
There may be two explanations for this answer. It may
be that Esau was accustomed to referring to God as
"your God," since he obviously did not regard Jehovah as his own God. If this was true, Jacob had to say it
this way to sound like Esau. The probable explanation
is that Jacob was afraid to involve God in his deceit.
He could not bring himself to say, "My God has
helped me." He sensed that when you go beyond the
bounds of godly propriety, you are on your own.
What he should have said was, "My mother
helped me."

And Isaac said unto Jacob, Come near, I pray thee, that I may feel thee, my son, whether thou be my very son Esau or not. And Jacob went near unto Isaac his father; and he felt him, and said, The voice is Jacob's voice, but the hands are the hands of Esau. And he discerned him not, because his hands were hairy, as his brother Esau's hands: so he blessed him. Genesis 27:21-23

Isaac was becoming blind, but he wasn't stupid. He said, "Come over here. Let me see you." He wanted to run his hands over those hairy arms and be sure that it was Esau.

When Jacob got near, Isaac detected that the voice was not Esau's, but Jacob's. Those who lose their sight gain a heightened sense of hearing and smell. He was perplexed when he felt Jacob's hands and arms. They seemed to him to be the hands and arms of Esau.

And he said, Art thou my very son Esau?
And he said, I am.
And he said, Bring it near to me, and I will eat of my son's venison, that my soul may bless thee. And he brought it near to him, and he did eat: and he brought him wine and he drank.
Genesis 27:24-25

But Isaac was not satisfied. "Are you really Esau?" he asked. Jacob was, again, forced to lie and affirm that he was Esau. He presented his father with the meal Rebekah had prepared, and Isaac ate it.

When Isaac had finished with the meal, he should have proceeded with the blessing, but something was still bothering him. Something didn't seem right. He asked Jacob to come near and kiss him. His intention was to see if he detected the smell of Esau, the smell of the field.

> *And his father Isaac said unto him, Come near now, and kiss me, my son. And he came near, and kissed him: and he smelled the smell of his raiment, and blessed him, and said, See, the smell of my son is as the smell of a field which the Lord hath blessed: Therefore God give thee of the dew of heaven, and the fatness of the earth, and plenty of corn and wine: Let people serve thee, and nations bow down to thee: be lord over thy brethren, and let thy mother's sons bow down to thee: cursed be every one that curseth thee, and blessed be he that blesseth thee.*   Genesis 27:26-29

When Jacob came near, Isaac took a long whiff, and, sure enough, this son had the smell of Esau. If he had the hands of Esau and the smell of Esau and knew how to cook like Esau, it must be Esau, Isaac thought. So, the plan worked, and Isaac was deceived.

When Isaac began to prophesy, therefore, he thought he was prophesy over Esau. But God knew exactly who was standing there in front of Isaac. The blessings spoken by Isaac had been destined for Jacob all along, because he had a heart toward God. And this blessing was not a duplication of what he had already received. This was something new.

The blessing spoke of *"the dew of heaven."* That meant that God was going to water his lands and make them productive.

The blessing mentioned: *"the fatness of the earth,"* and *"plenty of corn and wine."* God wants His people to prosper.

The blessing gave Jacob authority: *"Let people serve thee, and nations bow down to thee: be lord over thy brethren, and let thy mother's sons bow down to thee: cursed be every one that curseth thee, and blessed be he that blesseth thee."*

Thus, the birthright and the blessing were two distinct and separate blessings from God, the one having little or nothing to do with the other. The birthright was basically spiritual, and the blessing was basically physical.

When Esau returned from his hunt and came to present his father with the venison he had requested, both of them were deeply disturbed to realize that Esau had been preempted by Jacob and had lost his blessing.

> *And it came to pass, as soon as Isaac had made an end of blessing Jacob, and Jacob was yet scarce gone out from the presence of Isaac his father, that Esau his brother came in from his hunting. And he also had made savoury meat, and brought it unto his father, and said unto his father, Let my father arise, and eat of his son's venison, that thy soul*

*may bless me. And Isaac his father said unto him,
Who art thou? And he said, I am thy son, thy
firstborn Esau. And Isaac trembled very exceedingly, and said, Who? where is he that hath taken
venison, and brought it me, and I have eaten of all
before thou camest, and have blessed him? yea, and
he shall be blessed.*   Genesis 27:30-33

Isaac was shaken by this experience. He had loved
Esau so much and had hoped for the very best for him.
But, now he knew that Jacob would, indeed, be
blessed above his brother, and he was helpless to
change that fact. *"He shall be blessed,"* he said.

When the Lord has spoken, His word cannot be re-
called. Blessings which He has destined for us cannot
be diverted. Let the devil do what he wants, he cannot
hinder God's Word in our lives. Nothing can take
God's blessing from us. His purposes will be fulfilled,
regardless of the circumstances or regardless of what
men might do. When God blesses you, no one else can
curse you. When you have a heart toward God, His
blessing are guaranteed. *"He shall be blessed."* Claim
that promise as your own.

We have an inheritance in God. We are sons of God.
We are heirs of God. Healing is our bread. Let us take
what is rightfully ours. May the devil have nothing
that belongs to us.

Esau was greatly disturbed by this news:

*And when Esau heard the words of his father, he
cried with a great and exceeding bitter cry, and*

said unto his father, Bless me, even me also, O my
father.   Genesis 27:34

It hadn't bothered Esau to sell the birthright, but to
lose his physical inheritance was almost more than he
could bear. Both Isaac and Esau blamed Jacob.

And he said, Thy brother came with subtilty, and
hath taken away thy blessing. And he said, Is not
he rightly named Jacob? for he hath supplanted me
these two times: he took away my birthright; and,
behold, now he hath taken away my blessing.
                                    Genesis 27:35-36

It wasn't true, of course. Esau had willingly sold the
birthright. He put no value on it. If Jacob wanted it, he
could have it. What did he care about blessing future
generations? Now, we see that the blessing accompanied the birthright, a truth that we will explore in
greater detail later in the book. So, by forfeiting the
one, Esau lost both.

But Esau believed in the power of his father to bless.
He cried out to him:

And he said, Hast thou not reserved a blessing
for me?   Genesis 27:30-36

The Scriptures teach:

Believe in the Lord your God, so shall ye be estab-
lished; believe his prophets, so shall ye prosper.
                                    2 Chronicles 20:20

Isaac's response to the cry of his son was not very encouraging:

> *And Isaac answered and said unto Esau, Behold, I have made him thy lord, and all his brethren have I given to him for servants; and with corn and wine have I sustained him: and what shall I do now unto thee, my son?*   Genesis 27:37

By now, Esau was desperate. He saw his future going up in smoke. He realized that his sin was catching up with him. He wept, for the second time, and pleaded with his father to give him a blessing too — any blessing at all.

> *And Esau said unto his father, Hast thou but one blessing, my father? bless me, even me also, O my father. And Esau lifted up his voice, and wept.*
>   Genesis 27:38

The blessing Esau got, in response to this desperate plea, was mixed.

> *And Isaac his father answered and said unto him, Behold, thy dwelling shall be the fatness of the earth, and of the dew of heaven from above; And by thy sword shalt thou live, and shalt serve thy brother; and it shall come to pass when thou shalt have the dominion, that thou shalt break his yoke from off thy neck.*   Genesis 27:39-40

Not a very encouraging prospect! That day, Esau's hatred for his brother increased to the point that he was determined to kill Jacob.

> *And Esau hated Jacob because of the blessing wherewith his father blessed him: and Esau said in his heart, The days of mourning for my father are at hand; then will I slay my brother Jacob.*
> Genesis 27:41

The news of Esau's evil intentions got back to Rebekah and, through her, to Jacob.

> *And these words of Esau her elder son were told to Rebekah: and she sent and called Jacob her younger son, and said unto him, Behold, thy brother Esau, as touching thee, doth comfort himself, purposing to kill thee.* Genesis 27:42

Rebekah, ever the scheming mother, was now forced to plan Jacob's escape.

> *Now therefore, my son, obey my voice; and arise, flee thou to Laban my brother to Haran; And tarry with him a few days, until thy brother's fury turn away; Until thy brother's anger turn away from thee, and he forget that which thou hast done to him: then I will send, and fetch thee from thence: why should I be deprived also of you both in one day?* Genesis 27:43-45

Rebekah knew how to accomplish her plan. She planted a seed in the mind of Isaac.

> *And Rebekah said to Isaac, I am weary of my life because of the daughters of Heth: if Jacob take a wife of the daughters of Heth, such as these which are of the daughters of the land, what good shall my life do me?*   Genesis 27:46

Isaac responded in the way Rebekah had hoped. He sent for Jacob and advised him to go to Padanaram, the land of his mother's people, to seek a wife.

> *And Isaac called Jacob, and blessed him, and charged him, and said unto him, Thou shalt not take a wife of the daughters of Canaan. Arise, go to Padanaram, to the house of Bethuel thy mother's father; and take thee a wife from thence of the daughters of Laban thy mother's brother.*
>   Genesis 28:1-2

As Jacob was leaving home, Isaac prayed over him.

> *And God Almighty bless thee, and make thee fruitful, and multiply thee, that thou mayest be a multitude of people; And give thee the blessing of Abraham, to thee, and to thy seed with thee; that thou mayest inherit the land wherein thou art a stranger, which God gave unto Abraham. And Isaac sent away Jacob: and he went to Padanaram*

unto Laban, son of Bethuel the Syrian, the brother
of Rebekah, Jacob's and Esau's mother.

Genesis 28:3-5

This doesn't sound like a man in disfavor with God. It doesn't sound like a man in disobedience. It sounds very much like a man who is in the center of the will of God.

By this time, Isaac must have recognized the hand of God in everything that had happened. He must have seen the anger and bitterness of Esau; and he must have talked with God and received the assurance that he had not committed a serious blunder, but that God was working to bring His will to pass.

Nevertheless, the outcome was not a pleasant one for Jacob. He was forced to flee from home and to remain abroad for many years, not the few days that his mother had contemplated.

Chapter 3

Two Manner of People

And the Lord said unto her, Two nations are in thy womb, and two manner of people shall be separated from thy bowels; and the one people shall be stronger than the other people; and the elder shall serve the younger.   Genesis 25:23

Two boys could never be more different than were Jacob and Esau. They had the same grandparents, Abraham, called *"the father of faith," "the friend of God,"* and his wife, Sarah, a woman of faith in her own right. And the two boys had the same parents, Isaac and

Rebekah. Isaac, was a type of Christ. As Christ had been *"obedient unto death"* and *"opened not his mouth,"* Isaac had lain in obedience on the altar his father constructed on Mt. Moriah, ready to die. His only question to his father was, *"Where is the lamb?"* What a great spiritual heritage Jacob and Esau had!

How could two boys with the same parents and grandparents be so different? The answer is very simple. One of them wanted God, and the other didn't want anything to do with God. That made them so different that God called them *"two manner of people,"* and *"two nations."* They were so different that they were uncomfortable being together in their mother's womb. They couldn't wait to get out of there. A struggle had already begun that would last much of their lifetime.

There is always a struggle when darkness meets light, when good meets evil, when righteousness meets self. If you haven't experienced any struggles, you probably aren't letting your light shine as it ought to. Living for Jesus in this world produces struggles. He said:

> *If the world hate you, ye know that it hated me before it hated you. If ye were of the world, the world would love his own: but because ye are not of the world, but I have chosen you out of the world, therefore the world hateth you.*
>
> John 15:18-19

The struggle between Jacob and Esau was strengthened by the fact that the parents took sides, each "weighing in" in favor of a son: Isaac in favor of Esau, and Rebekah in favor of Jacob. The selling of the birthright should not have been cause to expand this struggle, because Esau willingly sold it, and Jacob willingly bought it. But, in a struggle of this type, no actual motive is needed; anything and everything causes conflict.

By agreeing to lie to and deceive his father, however, Jacob brought himself down to the level of his unbelieving brother and aggravated the division that would last for another twenty years. During that time, Jacob could never rest well at night, knowing that his brother was looking for him and wanted to kill him. What a terrible way to live!

As we shall see, the deceit served no good purpose. It only became a tool that Esau used against a brother he never hoped to understand. And how could he? The Apostle Paul declared:

> *What fellowship hath righteousness with unrighteousness? and what communion hath light with darkness? And what concord hath Christ with Belial? or what part hath he that believeth with an infidel? And what agreement hath the temple of God with idols? for ye are the temple of the living God; as God hath said, I will dwell in them, and walk in them; and I will be their God, and they shall be my people. Wherefore come out from among them, and be ye separate, saith the Lord, and touch not the unclean thing; and I will receive you.*   2 Corinthians 6:14-17

The struggle between the two manner of people still goes on today. It is not just the struggle between Jew and Arab, but the struggle between the saved and the lost, between the flesh and the Spirit, between right and wrong, between carnality and spirituality. It is a struggle that exists in every one of us, keeping many of us from being the leaders God has destined us to be.

Of this struggle, Paul wrote:

> *For the flesh lusteth against the Spirit, and the Spirit against the flesh: and these are contrary the one to the other: so that ye cannot do the things that ye would.*   Galatians 5:17

Jacob and Esau, God said, were *"two manner of people."*

The Sins of the Parents

> *And Isaac loved Esau, because he did eat of his venison: but Rebekah loved Jacob.*
> Genesis 25:28

The role of the parent in this struggle was significant. Isaac and Rebekah made a serious mistake in raising their twin sons, a serious mistake of which many parents of all generations have been guilty — that of loving one child more than another. Favoritism always causes problems for the offspring. If God gives us children, He expects us to love them all equally, as He does, and to demonstrate our love to each of them in the same way. If we fail to do that, it produces a division in the home.

The division in the household of Isaac and Rebekah showed up again and again.

And Isaac loved Esau, because he did eat of his venison: but Rebekah loved Jacob.
Genesis 25:28

Isaac loved his outdoorsman, and Rebekah loved the child who joyfully sat at her feet. It was this favoritism and the accompanying jealousy that favoritism invariably breeds that led Jacob to enter into a pact of deceit with his mother against his brother and against his father. Favoritism can never have a positive result.

Sometimes the reason a parent favors one child over another is that they see themselves in the other child and don't like what they see. But, whatever the reason, it is a dangerous practice. If God has given you children, love them all equally. Treat them all alike. Don't show favoritism. Don't give one of them more than another. Divide your favor evenly.

One father told me, "I have solved the problem with my two sons. When I have something to divide, I tell one of them to divide it, but I tell him to give his brother first choice. That way, I am sure that he will cut things right down the middle, so that the other will not get a fraction more than him."

Jacob was to later show favoritism to his own son, Joseph, and to cause much jealousy among his own sons. This all-too-common act always bears an evil harvest.

As parents, we are responsible before God to know our children and to understand their needs, and we cannot do that in the flesh. Carnal wisdom will never make proper parents. We need to hear from God. If we would spend more time hearing from God concerning our children we would know how to direct and encourage them. We cannot expect them to enjoy the same things we enjoy and to be interested in the same things in which we are interested. They are individuals, each different from the other.

What a terrible atmosphere these two boys grew up in: jealousy and bickering! No wonder Jacob was unable to control the same spirit in his own household in later life! The examples we give our children will affect coming generations — for good or for bad.

The diverging purposes of Isaac and Rebekah must have made for constant tension in the home. Isaac wanted Esau to succeed in life; but Rebekah wanted Jacob to succeed in life. What they couldn't see was that God wanted both Jacob and Esau to succeed and had prepared plenty of blessings to go around.

Rebekah was so bent on success for Jacob that she convinced him to lie and cheat to achieve his ends. And nothing good resulted from her conspiracy. It only engendered more hatred and mistrust between the two brothers.

Thank God that Isaac and Rebekah didn't do everything wrong. Isaac knew that what God had given to his father, Abraham, and to himself was for succeeding generations. He knew the value of what he had in God. He knew that he was blessed and was determined to pass that blessing on to his children. He knew that God was with him. He knew that he could impart something to his son, and he believed in imparting blessings through both prophecy and the laying on of hands.

Paul used these methods with his spiritual son, Timothy.

Wherefore I put thee in remembrance that thou stir up the gift of God, which is in thee by the putting on of my hands. 2 Timothy 1:6

Neglect not the gift that is in thee, which was given thee by prophecy, with the laying on of the hands of the presbytery. 1 Timothy 4:14

This charge I commit unto thee, son Timothy, according to the prophecies which went before on thee, that thou by them mightest war a good warfare; 1 Timothy 1:18

We can all use this form of blessing our children and others. God said in Ephesians:

Blessed be the God and Father of our Lord Jesus Christ, who hath blessed us with all spiritual blessings in heavenly places in Christ:
Ephesians 1:3

We are blessed with *"all spiritual blessings."* We are called to sit *"in heavenly places."* Let us learn to pass on those blessings. We are blessed, and we can bless others. God is with us, and His favor upon us can be "catching." Learn to bless those around you, as did the Patriarchs of old.

These are secrets that many modern-day parents have not yet discovered. Parents should lay hands on their children with regularity and impart God's blessings to them.

These good points about Isaac and Rebekah's treatment of their children did not erase the bad. They would pay for their failures in the continuing struggle between their two sons.

Chapter 4

Jacob Have I Loved

And not only this; but when Rebecca also had conceived by one, even by our father Isaac; (For the children being not yet born, neither having done any good or evil, that the purpose of God according to election might stand, not of works, but of him that calleth;) It was said unto her, The elder shall serve the younger. As it is written, Jacob have I loved, but Esau have I hated.   Romans 9:10-13

This is a most unusual passage of Scripture, for God is not in the hating business. He is Love (1 John 4:8).

What would cause a God of love, a God who *is* Love, to make such a dramatic statement? Is God even capable of hate? Is it possible for Him to hate? What does God hate? He certainly doesn't hate people; but He does hate sin. He hates any sin; He hates sin in anyone.

Knowing His love as we do, we would have to say that God didn't hate the person of Esau, but the sin of Esau. God was offended by Esau's spirit of rebellion and ungratefulness. He hated Esau's spirit of condescension. He hated the fact that Esau placed so little value on the spiritual and so much value on the physical. He hated the fact that Esau thought so little of tomorrow and so much of today. He hated the fact that Esau despised his birthright. He hated the fact that Esau did not want to be spiritual, that He did not want God Himself; for being spiritual is nothing more than loving God and loving the things of God.

God hates anything that separates a man from his Creator. He hates anything that robs us of our divine destiny in life.

God loved Jacob because Jacob wanted God. He wanted God's blessing on his life. He loved God's ways and God's words. He loved God's will. Esau, on the other hand, despised them all. God hated that.

When Jacob wrestled with the angel, he said, "I will not let you go until you bless me." God loved that about Jacob.

This special favor with God for certain individuals is clearly outlined in the Bible. Jesus, for instance, had a special love for the disciple John. John is pictured resting his head upon the bosom of the Lord. But it wasn't that Jesus loved John more than the other disciples. It was that John loved Jesus and wanted to be close to Him.

That seems radical to many people. They don't understand it when you love Jesus more than anything else. They think you are a little strange. They look at you carefully and wonder if you might even be dangerous. But, don't worry about it. If you love the Lord, He will cause you to prosper — whatever others do and say.

> *The blessing of the Lord, it maketh rich, and he addeth no sorrow with it.* Proverbs 10:22

When my father passed away in 1972, he had twenty dollars in his pocket. He had spent his whole lifetime helping people find God. He had nothing to leave us, materially speaking; but he left us the greatest treasures that anybody could possibly hope for in life — faith in God and liberty in the Holy Ghost. Those were his legacies to us. He taught us that if we would only walk in faith and in the power of the Holy Ghost the world would be ours. How foolish we would be to take those things lightly!

He lived the example of faith before us. When he was sick, he didn't run to the doctor. He believed God for his own healing. And his faith was contagious. We caught it.

So many pastors today are the first in line at the doctor's office. That is why they have no faith to pray for the healing of their members. What must their members think when the pastor preaches about faith? That is why many preachers have stopped preaching faith entirely.

My mother is more than eighty years old, and she has never been to a doctor, and never taken medicine. She still doesn't need glasses to read. While we were growing up, she never gave us medicines. She trusted God. She taught us to trust in Dr. Jesus for our own healing.

Those teachings have never left us:

> *Train up a child in the way he should go: and when he is old, he will not depart from it.*
>
> Proverbs 22:6

Jacob had a heart toward God. He felt like David:

> *As the hart panteth after the water brooks, so panteth my soul after thee, O God.*   Psalms 42:1

Paul understood that. He cried out:

> *That I may know him, and the power of his resurrection, and the fellowship of his sufferings, being made conformable unto his death;*
>
> Philippians 3:10

Knowing God and understanding Him better are the major goals of all those who have a heart toward God. And we are not the strange ones. Our love for Jesus is entirely normal, and it pleases Him.

God hates it when people ignore His love. He is the Creator of the Universe. Without Him, nothing at all would exist. He is the one that gives us life and breath. How can we not love Him?

When our heart is set upon Him, He becomes the principal motivation for our lives. If, on the other hand, we look primarily to other sources, they become our motivation instead. This is why Jesus said:

> *But seek ye first the kingdom of God, and his righteousness; and all these things shall be added unto you.* Matthew 6:33

When the motivation is right, everything else will follow. If the motivation is wrong, we are doomed to failure. I wouldn't trade the anointing of God for all the beautiful mansions I saw in Palm Beach, Florida. I wouldn't sell the blessing of God for the Rolls Royce automobile I saw or for the more expensive Mercedes models that cost $100,000 and up. I love the Lord, and I know that He loves me. What money could buy that blessing?

The Lord loves sinners, but His love for those who have chosen to walk with Him is even a much greater manifestation. He loves us in a special way.

Esau rejected God's love. He rejected God's love for himself, for his family, and for his nation. He rejected, as being unimportant, his privileges as the firstborn of the family. He counted as expendable his spiritual authority. He had another agenda. God said of him:

Follow peace with all men, and holiness, without which no man shall see the Lord: Looking diligently lest any man fail of the grace of God; lest any root of bitterness springing up trouble you, and thereby many be defiled; Lest there be any fornicator, or profane person, as Esau, who for one morsel of meat sold his birthright. For ye know how that afterward, when he would have inherited the blessing, he was rejected: for he found no place of repentance, though he sought it carefully with tears.   Hebrews 12:14-17

God considered Esau to be a *"profane person"*; he lacked *"holiness."* What does holiness mean? It means living a life pleasing to the Lord. It means pleasing Him on the inside (in our thought life and the intents of our hearts), and it means pleasing Him on the outside, as well. Some people have an outward appearance of holiness but are meaner than snakes. Get the inward, and get the outward too.

Esau was a *"profane person."* He lacked *"holiness."* And, because of it, he was rejected of God. What could be worse than to be rejected by God? Too late Esau apparently realized what he had lost. Too late he realized the value of the blessing he had sold for a *"morsel."* Like so many, he learned to value of what God had given him, but too late.

He realized too late how foolish he had been. When tomorrow arrived, he learned that tomorrow is important, and that we always pay for the sins of yesterday. He was sorry and wept, but was he sorry for the right reasons? Only God can judge that, and God rejected his tears.

To me, that means that Esau was not truly repentant. God is a God of mercy. He is always ready to forgive those who repent and turn to Him. I believe that the only reason Esau changed his mind and *"sought a place of repentance"* was because of the material wealth he would be losing. His father, now near death, was rich in cattle and lands and servants and gold and silver; and Esau couldn't bear to lose all that. He also couldn't bear to become spiritual, so God rejected him. The prosperity that God has destined for His people rests upon a prosperity of the soul. The birthright and the blessing go together.

> *Beloved, I wish above all things that thou mayest prosper and be in health, even as thy soul prospereth.*   3 John 1:2

When our hearts and minds are toward God, His blessings come to us automatically. God has promised to bless us. We were not meant to be beneath the people of the world. If we earn the same as they do, and pay our tithes and avoid bad habits, our money should go further than theirs. We should prosper financially. It is God's perfect will for us.

The prophet Malachi also spoke of God's feeling for Jacob and against Esau:

> *The burden of the word of the Lord to Israel by Malachi. I have loved you, saith the Lord. Yet ye*

> *say, Wherein hast thou loved us? Was not Esau*
> *Jacob's brother? saith the Lord: yet I loved Jacob,*
> *And I hated Esau, and laid his mountains and his*
> *heritage waste for the dragons of the wilderness.*
> *Whereas Edom saith, We are impoverished, but we*
> *will return and build the desolate places; thus*
> *saith the Lord of hosts, They shall build, but I will*
> *throw down; and they shall call them, the border of*
> *wickedness, and, the people against whom the*
> *Lord hath indignation for ever. And your eyes*
> *shall see, and ye shall say, The Lord will be magni-*
> *fied from the border of Israel.*   Malachi 1:1-5

Because of Esau's rejection of the things of God, God vowed that he would not ultimately prosper. If he built up his waste places, God would destroy them again. You simply cannot reject God and expect to prosper.

There is some Bible precedent for the firstborn rejecting the birthright. The first man, Adam, was carnal. The second man Adam was spiritual. Adam's first son, Cain, wanted nothing to do with God and killed his brother in jealousy. Saul, the first king of Israel, despised the will of God and lost his throne. He was followed by David, a man *after God's own heart*. Israel, the original branch, rejected God and was cut off. Now, the Church has been grafted into the vine.

Esau responded to his own failure in a very typical way. He blamed his brother for everything and determined to take vengeance on him.

And he [Isaac] said, Thy brother came with subtilty, and hath taken away thy blessing. And he [Esau] said, Is not he rightly named Jacob? for he hath supplanted me these two times: he took away my birthright; and, behold, now he hath taken away my blessing. And he said, Hast thou not reserved a blessing for me?

Genesis 27:35-36

And Esau hated Jacob because of the blessing wherewith his father blessed him: and Esau said in his heart, The days of mourning for my father are at hand; then will I slay my brother Jacob.

Genesis 27:41

So many people are filled with hate. They hate everyone and everything. They are unusually angry about their own failures in life. But, since they can't bring themselves to admit that they have erred and can't bring themselves to genuine repentance, they blame everyone else for their failure.

Esau was positive that he had lost because Jacob had stolen his birthright. That was not true, however. Esau lost the birthright because he didn't value it and because he sold it in exchange for temporary gratification. He lost it because of a lack of faith in its value. Later, he blamed everyone else for his own failure.

The second thing Esau did was to take spiteful action against his parents. When he heard that his mother was grieved because he had married pagan wives and that his father had sent Jacob away to find a

wife among his mother's family, he rushed right out
and, in defiance of his parents wishes, married another unbelieving women, his third wife.

> *When Esau saw that Isaac had blessed Jacob, and*
> *sent him away to Padanaram, to take him a wife*
> *from thence; and that as he blessed him he gave*
> *him a charge, saying, Thou shalt not take a wife of*
> *the daughters of Canaan; And that Jacob obeyed*
> *his father and his mother, and was gone to*
> *Padanaram; And Esau seeing that the daughters*
> *of Canaan pleased not Isaac his father; Then went*
> *Esau unto Ishmael, and took unto the wives which*
> *he had Mahalath the daughter of Ishmael*
> *Abraham's son, the sister of Nebajoth, to be*
> *his wife.*   Genesis 28:6-9

In rejecting his parents, Esau was rejecting God — as
he had done consistently. He had not only failed to
repent, he was further hardening his heart against
God. God wanted to be Esau's Friend; God wanted to
be Esau's Protector; and God wanted to be Esau's Sup-
plier. But Esau would have none of it.

Esau *"would have inherited the blessing."* He *would
have*, but he didn't. God rejected his tears. God rejected
his repentance. It was improperly motivated by a desire for earthly gain, not a desire to make heaven his
home and be a blessing to all the nations of the earth.

God was directing Isaac in his blessing. He could
have prevented the deception. He knew that it was
Jacob standing before his father and not Esau. No one

can fool God. Yet, he gave Isaac the words of blessing that He had already determined for Jacob.

Once, when I was ministering in Australia, some preachers decided to attend without telling anyone who they were. They wanted to see if God had a word for them. When they came forward, they were dressed just like a farmer who was standing beside them and just like a legal assistant who was standing on the other side. But they couldn't fool God. He knew exactly who they were and gave them a word commensurate with their position and their need.

I was invited to minister to a group of very wealthy ladies. When I began to prophesy over them, I was amazed at what the Lord was saying. Looking at those ladies with the natural eye, one would have supposed that, with the income level they enjoyed and the level of education they possessed, they would have had relatively few problems in life, but that wasn't true. God knows all about us. We can't fool Him. He knew that Jacob was standing there and not Esau, so he spoke forth Jacob's blessing.

Jacob was blessed because he had a heart toward God. If Esau had repented and genuinely sought God at any moment, forgiveness would have been forthcoming immediately. God is merciful. Esau, however, was sorry only because he had lost his fortune.

There are many lessons to this. One of them counters the popular teaching that is being disseminated widely these days that it is foolish to try to please God, that because He has already done everything for us, we need do nothing for Him.

The fact that God loved Jacob and hated Esau shows that it is possible to live a life pleasing to God, and there are attitudes and acts that God hates. He loves those who live for Him. He hates it when men and women ignore His will — for any reason.

God rejected Esau, because Esau had rejected God. Like many people, he wanted the fringe benefits without paying the price.

Love the Blesser, and the blessings will come.

Part II

Jacob and Esau:
Contrasts In Leadership

Chapter 5

Esau's Carnality and Jacob's Spirituality

There is therefore now no condemnation to them which are in Christ Jesus, who walk not after the flesh, but after the Spirit. For the law of the Spirit of life in Christ Jesus hath made me free from the law of sin and death. For what the law could not do, in that it was weak through the flesh, God sending his own Son in the likeness of sinful flesh, and for sin, condemned sin in the flesh: That the righteousness of the law might be fulfilled in us, who walk not after the flesh, but after the Spirit. For they that are after the flesh do mind the things of the flesh; but they that are after the Spirit the things of the Spirit. For to be carnally minded is death; but to be spiritually minded is life and peace.   Romans 8:1-6

Esau was carnal. He was more concerned with satisfying the flesh than with anything of lasting value. This fact is reflected most powerfully in the selling of the birthright.

When it happened, he was returning from the fields; and, because he was a good hunter, it seems logical to suppose that he had some game with him that he had just killed. But he couldn't wait for it to be dressed and prepared. He was hungry NOW. He had to be satisfied NOW. Would he sell his birthright for a temporal blessing? Surely not. Or would he?

He told Jacob that he had to have the meal because he was *"at the point to die."* Was he really at the point of death, or was he just hungry? It probably didn't matter to him. In his thinking, being hungry was equivalent to being near death. He couldn't stand it. For too many years he had live a life of carnality, giving the flesh what it demanded. He wasn't about to stop now. He would rather sell something of future value to satisfy a momentary desire than wait until his own game could be dressed and cooked.

Isn't it interesting how desperate the flesh gets! It just has to find expression or it will "die."

Esau was faint. He was tired. I understand that. He was just human, like the rest of us. I get tired sometimes, and you will get tired too. I feel faint sometimes, and you will feel faint sometimes too. We are all human. But feeling tired or faint is no excuse for coddling the flesh.

When we are into our summer camp activities at our campground in Virginia, our people get up early and stay up late every day for more than ten weeks. There is a lot of work to be done to make the camp comfortable for those who come from all over the world to be blessed by God. There are many responsibilities: the shopping, the cooking, the cleaning, and the serving, to mention only a few. Then, many of those same people who do those jobs participate in the ministry to hungry hearts, something that can go on into the wee hours of the night.

With so much to be done, it is not surprising that they should get tired. But, because they are willing to lay aside their own comfort in order to be a blessing to others, God has blessed our camp workers in unusual ways and used them all over the world.

It is not a sin to get tired, but it is a sin to use tiredness as an excuse to sin. Even Paul knew what it was to be *"weak."*

> *For his letters, say they, are weighty and powerful; but his bodily presence is weak, and his speech contemptible.*   2 Corinthians 10:10

> *Therefore I take pleasure in infirmities, in reproaches, in necessities, in persecutions, in distresses for Christ's sake: for when I am weak, then am I strong.*   2 Corinthians 12:10

Paul was not overcome by his weakness but found his strength in Christ. Weakness is not a bad thing, in this sense. It teaches us to open ourselves to the Holy Ghost and to depend on Him.

Soon after I was saved, I began helping my father work on the campground. There was much to be done, and he worked us night and day, until I felt exhausted. One night, in church service, I was hoping that my mother would not call on me to pray when the singing was finished, but I was afraid that she might. I was just too tired that night.

"Let her call on someone else," I prayed. "I can hardly stand up, let alone lead in prayer."

But, just as soon as the singing was finished, Mother called on me to pray — just as I sensed that she would. As I opened my mouth to pray, I was crying out of my spirit for the Lord to help ME, and He did. I had never prayed a more anointed prayer. Before I was finished, people were shouting and praising God, and I wasn't tired anymore.

Our bodies get tired; but, thank God, He is always there to strengthen us. He never needs sleep.

> *Behold, he that keepeth Israel shall neither slumber nor sleep.*   Psalms 121:4

When we learn to tap into the anointing of the Holy Ghost, it doesn't matter how long or how hard we have worked. We are able to stand in His strength and not faint. If we haven't learned this lesson, however, we become easy targets for the Enemy.

Many believers need days or even weeks to prepare, to strengthen themselves, before they can do anything in the church. But this is not good. There is too much to be done. We must be prepared at all times. We must stand constantly in the glory of the Lord.

Some, because they are physically tired, always minimize what they are going to do before they get started. They say, "You'll have to forgive me. I have a terrible cold. My singing won't be very good tonight. Please bear with me, and just listen to the message of the words."

Don't make excuses. Just stand in the strength of the Lord and feed His people. If you only have canned Spam, make it taste like roast beef. Don't let the weariness of the flesh overcome you and destroy your effectiveness.

Prophecy is becoming increasingly popular these days. Everyone wants to prophesy — a little. But when it comes to declaring the word of the Lord to dozens of hungry hearts, hour after hour, night after night, few are willing to pay that price.

Sometimes, as you minister, you may feel you have no more strength, that everything has been "wrung out of you," yet you still have eight people standing in line to be ministered to. You have already been standing there for two hours or more, but you are not yet finished. The people even seem to multiply. As some are blessed, others take their place in line, hoping to receive their word from the Lord, as well.

You may feel that you have nothing else to give, but that is not a bad feeling. You are not ministering of yourself; and, if you recognize from the very beginning that you have nothing to offer, you will rely more fully on the Lord; and He never fails.

I have found that sometimes those last ones in the line, perhaps because they have been standing there so long, actually get the very best word. An unusual refreshing comes down from heaven, and the Lord shows us that He is indeed Lord, and that nothing is too hard for Him. If there is an empty vessel waiting to be filled, and you are willing to minister to that vessel, God will give you something to pour out. Don't ever let physical limitations keep you from God's best.

There are two variables that have great influence in the operation of the gifts of the Spirit: the need that exists, and your willingness and desire to respond to that need. Nothing else is important.

> *Withhold not good from them to whom it is due,*
> *when it is in the power of thine hand to do it.*
> Proverbs 3:27

If you have no desire to minister healing to sick people, you will never receive the anointing to do so. God doesn't force His gifts on you. When the compassion of Christ begins to be stirred up within you on behalf of the sick and suffering, God will begin to move through you to bring healing and deliverance to them.

Esau's problem wasn't tiredness. He just used that as an excuse. His problem was that he had no desire to be spiritual. He had no desire to be the priest of his family. Esau's problem was Esau. Weakness was just the tool that Satan used to rob him.

When you are weak, your senses seem to sharpen. Esau smelled that good food cooking, and his senses overpowered him. The senses constitute a danger zone for all believers.

Another is the desire to buy more "things." In recent years, we have experienced such prosperity in America that everyone seems to be looking for something else worth buying. Everyone seems to be buying a boat or buying a bigger boat. Everyone seems to be shopping for a car or a better car. Everyone seems to be looking for ways to satisfy their flesh. Will we never learn that the flesh has an insatiable appetite and cannot ever be satisfied? Solomon learned that lesson the hard way.

> *I have seen all the works that are done under the sun; and, behold, all is vanity and vexation of spirit.*   Ecclesiastes 1:14

We were not created to be satisfied with anything less than the fullness of the presence of the Lord. He is our source. Look to Him.

The flesh leads us to do some very foolish things. A few years before I got saved, I bought a new 1960 Pontiac. It was solid white outside, with a red and black interior. I thought it was the most gorgeous car I had ever seen. I bought it in Cincinnati and drove all the way back to Lexington, Kentucky, just to show it to my friends. They were happy for me. Then, I remember waking up the next morning to the realization that I had thirty-six months of payments ahead of me and wondering if I had done the right thing.

We are so fickle. Our flesh tells us that we must buy one of those giant screen television sets. "After all, it's just like going to the movies." And if it wasn't that, it would be something else. Flesh is never happy. There is always something else, usually something very expensive and difficult to acquire, that we are sure will make us happy, if we can only find a way to acquire it.

Esau made his choice and had no one to blame but himself. He refused to be spiritual and had to pay the cost. Every Jewish woman prayed to be blessed with the privilege of bringing forth the Messiah; and most every Jewish father would have been proud to be part of the lineage of the Savior, but not Esau. He was too selfish.

It is very possible that Esau appeared to be religious to his friends. Many people of his status use religion as a means of moving up the ladder. Being religious is a smart social move for them. But simply being religious is not enough. Being religious and being spiritual are not the same. I know people who are very religious, more religious than most of us. Some would say that they are "very sincere." I agree. They are sincere, but they are on their way to hell, nevertheless — if they haven't accepted Jesus as their Lord and Savior.

Nobody is more sincere than a dedicated Muslim. Nobody is more sincere than a dedicated Buddhist. Nobody is more sincere than a dedicated Hindu. A poor Hindu will give his last food in sacrifice to one of the many gods he serves. Compared to the countries dominated by these religions, America is really not very religious at all. Those who follow these religions are obviously in error. They don't yet know Jesus, and many of them have never had the opportunity to do so. The sad thing is to see many Americans who have had every opportunity to hear the Gospel and who maintain a religious front of sorts, but who have never attained to spirituality.

In India, with its 800 million inhabitants, everyone has a god. There are at least 330,000 different gods there. Some Indians worship insects. Some of them worship trees. Some of them worship monkeys and other animals. Some of them worship the dead. They worship everything. They are very religious people.

In America today, only forty to forty-five percent of our population even attends church, and many of those who do attend only go on Easter or Christmas or to funerals. Compared to the Buddhist countries, we are not a very religious people. In the Moslem and Hindu countries, most everyone has some form of worship. Our American gods have become money, success, pleasure, and possessions.

Troubles are coming to America that will cause us to return to the true and living God and cry out to Him for salvation. Some people will come to Him no other way. But why wait for trouble to come? It is time to lay aside carnality and to develop a living relationship with the Lord Jesus Christ.

Many people believe that Jacob was wrong for taking advantage of the weakness of Esau and bargaining, as he did, for the birthright. I don't agree. I think he was just an enterprising businessman who knew the value of the birthright, saw that his brother didn't appreciate its worth, and looked for an opportunity to put that knowledge to work.

Seeing Esau's weakness, he pressed his advantage and won. He didn't trust his brother much and made him swear that he would keep this agreement. And Esau didn't have a problem with that.

> *And Jacob said, Swear to me this day; And he sware unto him: and he sold his birthright unto Jacob.*   Genesis 25:33

So few words to summarize such a great tragedy! In exchange for a few lentils and some bread, a spiritual heritage changed hands. Esau refused to be spiritual. He despised his birthright. He said:

> *What profit shall this birthright do to me?*
>   Genesis 25:32

No wonder the Scriptures call him a *"profane person."* Anyone who would take his heritage so lightly is not worthy of respect. And yet the world looks up to the Esau types, believing that they have great personal fulfillment. It is not true. We usually don't know about the heartache and suffering that exist in their lives. We usually don't know what happens behind those closed doors. We do know that the blessing of the Lord makes us rich; and that is enough.

Esau wept bitterly when he learned that Jacob had taken his blessing.

And when Esau heard the words of his father, he cried with a great and exceeding bitter cry, and said unto his father, Bless me, even me also, O my father.   Genesis 27:34

Tears are often a sign of repentance, but Esau didn't shed a single tear when he sold his spiritual birthright. It meant nothing to him. Now, when he knew that his brother would be blessed physically too, he wept. Those are not the kind of tears that move the heart of God.

Giving away his right to be priest of the family was nothing to Esau. Giving away his right to bless the earth was nothing to him. Now he wept, but he had no one to blame but himself. He had, after all, been born first. He had the automatic right to the privileges of the firstborn. If he had not sold the birthright, there would have been no question as to whom it belonged. The line of succession was Abraham, Isaac, and Esau. That succession changed forever the day he sold his most valuable possession — his spiritual heritage.

He hadn't minded that the promise to provide the godly line which would be used to bring into the world the future Messiah had been forfeited to his brother. That was nothing to him. What good did a future Messiah do him? He didn't shed a single tear that day. It was the thought of losing land and cattle and servants that bothered Esau and made him weep.

People weep over different things, don't they? Some weep when their health is lost; others weep when their fortune is gone; still others weep when their family disintegrates. But how very few of us weep for souls these days! What moves you?

It is time to choose to be spiritual. I can't make you spiritual, and you can't make me spiritual. The desire must come from within. There must be a yearning, a desire, a longing to come into a relationship with Jesus and to do what God has called us to do. We have to empty ourselves of self so that God can work in us, to make room for that which God wants to give every one of us.

David prayed:

> *Cast me not away from thy presence; and take not thy holy spirit from me. Restore unto me the joy of thy salvation; and uphold me with thy free spirit.*
>   Psalms 51:11-12

We each need to press into a new place, a greater place, in God than we have experienced until now, so that we might see the lives of many men and women changed by God.

When you choose to be spiritual, you may be misunderstood by others. Some may not like you because you are spiritual. Your spirituality shows up their lack of spirituality. They don't feel comfortable around you because you want to live for God and be holy. Don't worry. If God is with you, nothing else matters.

The Devil's attack against Esau was so typical of his tactics. He never tries to conquer us all at once. He just nips away at our heels, trying to tire us until he can "come in for the kill." He tells us that one little sin won't harm us. He never suggests that we backslide and go away from God. He tells us that a little sin won't separate us from God, that God will "understand." Those who fall for these lies pay the inevitable consequences.

We have a lot of carnal Christians today. They want to go to church as if it were a club. And they want people to know that they go to church, that they have a form of religion. Some of them are born again, but that is far enough for them; they have no desire to go deeper in the things of the Spirit.

Carnal people often act like children. We have those who go around casting devils out of each other, when the truth is that those people out of whom the demons are supposedly being cast just need more of God. You can't cast out the works of the flesh. You have to develop works of the Spirit to replace them. It is time to grow up and act like mature and responsible believers.

Many Christians are totally satisfied with a form of religion. They want to walk with one foot in the church and the other in the world. That is a very dangerous practice. God says:

> *Wherefore come out from among them, and be ye separate, saith the Lord, and touch not the unclean thing; and I will receive you.*
> 2 Corinthians 6:17

It is time to stop dabbling in the world and get serious with God. Many carnal Christians will not make it to heaven. And who is to blame? I don't blame the average church member. I blame preachers who are not preaching the whole Gospel and other church leaders who are not willing to live it.

There is no conviction in many of our churches. People can go there and feel comfortable and still continue to live in sin. For the most part, they don't like to feel conviction. They don't understand that the convicting power of the Holy Ghost is a wonderful thing, wonderful to let the Lord show us the things that are not pleasing to Him. It is wonderful to let Him reveal to us that which is preventing Him from moving in our lives.

The sermons you might hear in such churches are well-outlined and beautifully presented. All the proper homiletical points are being struck, and what is being said makes you feel good but puts no conviction in your soul.

We are too close to home to play church. The New World Order is in place. The world is more ready for the coming of the Anti-Christ than the Church is for the coming of Jesus. Rise up, saints of God. Only the *"pure in heart"* will see Him.

> *Blessed are the pure in heart: for they shall see God.*   Matthew 5:8

Let the Lord bring His convicting power in your life and make you spiritual. He has given us each a great responsibility, and we must strive for spirituality, not only to please God, but to set an example for others to follow.

The Devil will dangle anything at all in your sight to make your head turn, to get your eyes off the goal and away from the path. He doesn't want you to look to God. Make up your mind that nothing will distract you, nothing will hinder you, nothing will turn you aside from the goal of spirituality.

Chapter 6

Esau's Impatience and Concern With the Present and Jacob's Patience and Concern With the Future

Wherefore seeing we also are compassed about with so great a cloud of witnesses, let us lay aside every weight, and the sin which doth so easily beset us, and let us run with patience the race that is set before us,　　　　Hebrews 12:1

Esau wanted what smelled good, and he wanted it NOW. He couldn't wait, even for a little while. He had his own game to prepare, but he couldn't wait that long. He must be satisfied NOW. He felt faint and wanted what he wanted, NOW. This impatience and preoccupation with the present spoiled his future.

A man of Esau's type would not have refused the respect and authority that came with being the priest of the family. The problem Esau had with accepting the position was that he could not become priest of his family until the death of his father, and he could not wait for his time. If he couldn't have it NOW, then it wasn't worth having. If he was going to get something, he wanted it NOW.

He couldn't be bothered with the thought of being progenitor of some future Messiah. What good was a future Messiah, when he was hungry and faint NOW?

Impatience is a thief. If something is worth having, it is worth waiting for. Don't let the Devil push you into doing something you will later regret. So many young men and women rush off and get married because they won't wait for the mate God has prepared for them. They are not satisfied with the timing of God. Most Christians are not happy with the trials and tests they must pass in order to reach their goals. They would prefer to take a short cut, to bypass the trials and troubles and get right to the blessings.

God has a right to test you to see what kind of stuff you are made of. If you can't stand the test of time, God can't trust you with eternity. Esau wasn't willing to wait.

The New Testament has much to say about patience. Among its treasures are the following:

In your PATIENCE possess ye your souls.
                                        Luke 21:19

We glory in tribulations also: knowing that tribulation worketh PATIENCE;   Romans 5:3

But if we hope for that we see not, then do we with PATIENCE wait for it.   Romans 8:25

For whatsoever things were written aforetime were written for our learning, that we through PATIENCE and comfort of the scriptures might have hope.   Romans 15:4

But in all things approving ourselves as the ministers of God, in much PATIENCE, in afflictions, in necessities, in distresses,   2 Corinthians 6:4

Truly the signs of an apostle were wrought among you in all PATIENCE, in signs, and wonders, and mighty deeds.   2 Corinthians 12:12

Strengthened with all might, according to his glorious power, unto all PATIENCE and longsuffering with joyfulness;
                                        Colossians 1:11

Remembering without ceasing your work of faith, and labour of love, and PATIENCE of hope in our Lord Jesus Christ, in the sight of God and our Father;   1 Thessalonians 1:3

*So that we ourselves glory in you in the churches
of God for your PATIENCE and faith in all your
persecutions and tribulations that ye endure:*
2 Thessalonians 1:4

*But thou, O man of God, flee these things; and
follow after righteousness, godliness, faith, love,
PATIENCE, meekness.*   1 Timothy 6:11

*That ye be not slothful, but followers of them who
through faith and PATIENCE inherit the
promises.*   Hebrews 6:12

*For ye have need of PATIENCE, that, after ye
have done the will of God, ye might receive the
promise.*   Hebrews 10:36

*Knowing this, that the trying of your faith
worketh PATIENCE. But let PATIENCE have
her perfect work, that ye may be perfect and entire,
wanting nothing.*   James 1:3-4

*Be patient therefore, brethren, unto the coming of
the Lord. Behold, the husbandman waiteth for the
precious fruit of the earth, and hath long PA-
TIENCE for it, until he receive the early and
latter rain.*   James 5:7

*Take, my brethren, the prophets, who have spoken
in the name of the Lord, for an example of suffering affliction, and of PATIENCE. Behold, we*

count them happy which endure. Ye have heard of the PATIENCE of Job, and have seen the end of the Lord; that the Lord is very pitiful, and of tender mercy. James 5:10-11

And to knowledge temperance; and to temperance PATIENCE; and to PATIENCE godliness;
2 Peter 1:6

I know thy works, and thy labour, and thy PATIENCE ... And hast borne, and hast PATIENCE, and for my name's sake hast laboured, and hast not fainted. Revelation 2:2-3

I know thy works, and charity, and service, and faith, and thy PATIENCE ... .
Revelation 2:19

"What good is this birthright to me?" Esau asked. It had no present value to him; it didn't immediately resolve his hunger and his tiredness; and he was not a man capable of seeing value in anything future. He lived only for today.

No wonder he was an easy sell! It is very easy for a good salesman to take advantage of such a person. If you are looking at a house to buy, and the real estate agent tells you that six other people are interested in that house, you think, *I'd better buy this now, before someone else gets it.*

You should ask yourself first, "If six other people want that house, why has it been sitting on the market for six weeks?" Good salesmen know how to use our impatience to their benefit. Jacob had seen his brother's lack of patience and was just biding his time for an opportunity he was sure to come at some point, when he could set his own price for the treasured birthright.

The prophet Habakkuk said:

> *For the vision is yet for an appointed time, but at the end it shall speak, and not lie: though it tarry, wait for it; because it will surely come, it will not tarry.*   Habakkuk 2:3

Impatience is a thief. God will move in His time. Don't get impatient. Don't throw up your hands in defeat. Don't throw the towel into the ring. Don't do something you will be sorry for later. Wait on God. Wait for the vision He gave you.

Momentary pleasure, momentary satisfaction, is deceitful. It doesn't pay off for the long haul. It isn't worth it. When we make sudden decisions based on our feelings at the moment, we are often sorry later, when we have had more time to think the thing through. Don't get in a hurry. Wait on God. Learn the value of moving in God's perfect time, and learn to live not just for the moment but with your eyes on eternity.

Chapter 7

Esau's Unwillingness to Sacrifice and Jacob's Readiness To Do Whatever Was Necessary

The Spirit itself beareth witness with our spirit, that we are the children of God: And if children, then heirs; heirs of God, and joint-heirs with Christ; if so be that we suffer with him, that we may be also glorified together. For I reckon that the sufferings of this present time are not worthy to be compared with the glory which shall be revealed in us. Romans 8:16-18

The Jews believe that Esau would never have been a good leader because he was not willing to suffer. Anyone who is not willing to pay a price for that which God has called him or her to do, anyone who wants everything to come easily, anyone who refuses to face trials and hardships, will fail to achieve greatness in God.

Many people never get promoted on their jobs because they just can't wait until quitting time to punch the clock. They feel they "just have" to leave early. The people who get promoted are those who come in a little early and stay late to finish their work, putting the good of the company ahead of their own comfort.

I am not happy about the many jobs that have been lost in America, many of them in the steel and auto and textile industries; but many American workers have nobody but themselves to blame. If they had stopped looking at the clock all day and started accomplishing something, America wouldn't have fallen behind in productivity; and many of our factories wouldn't have closed.

Many of those same people would be happy now to have even part time work. They would be satisfied to take less pay now than they were making before. They now wish they had worked harder and been more conscientious. But it's too late. Great companies are built on sacrifice. If Asians or Latin Americans are willing to sacrifice, they will get the available jobs.

Esau was not willing to suffer, even for a moment, so he lost his place of leadership. Moses became a great leader because he was willing to be identified with his people and to suffer with them.

By faith Moses, when he was come to years, re-
fused to be called the son of Pharaoh's daughter;
Choosing rather to suffer affliction with the people
of God, than to enjoy the pleasures of sin for a
season; Esteeming the reproach of Christ greater
riches than the treasures in Egypt: for he had re-
spect unto the recompence of the reward.
Hebrews 11:24-26

Moses witnessed an Egyptian killing a Hebrew. When he saw that, he forgot that he was in line to become the Pharaoh and got involved with the problems of his people. He chose to be identified with the hated Hebrews and killed that Egyptian.

If you hope to hold a position of leadership in God's Kingdom, you must identify with God's people. You must be willing to jump in, wherever and whenever you see a need, and to stand shoulder to shoulder with others, to share the burden and help carry the load. When you do that, people will respect you and look up to you. Until that day, you must go about the process of earning people's respect.

When I was in the army, we had a sergeant who loved to party on weekends. When our company commander said that if any barracks won the prize for cleanliness and neatness during inspection three out of five days during the week, the soldiers of that barracks would have the weekend off, that sergeant said, "Boys, I don't plan to work even one weekend. We are going to win that prize." But he did the right thing: he not only taught us what was necessary to pass inspection; he jumped in and worked with us to achieve the goal. I saw him get on his hands and knees to clean the latrines; and, sure enough, seven out of eight weeks, we won the prize and had our weekends free.

That's the kind of leadership we need in the Church today. Too many leaders are saying to their people, "Don't do as I do; do as I say." But it doesn't work that way. We must be the examples of what we are teaching. We cannot expect anyone to sacrifice more than we are willing to sacrifice ourselves.

We have too many chiefs in the Church and not enough Indians. Everybody wants to boss somebody else. What we need to do is show people how to do things by doing them ourselves. Let us be willing to get our hands dirty for God. Stop criticizing everyone else. Jump in, and get the job done.

We often have to send out large mailings relating to our camp activities. Anyone who has done it will tell you that it is a LOT of work to get out 17,000 pieces of mail. One person can't do it, and neither can two or even three people. It takes a team effort. We always get a couple of long tables lined up. Then we all get around and help until the job is done. Even then, it takes a couple of full days of concentrated effort, but it can be done.

When I had a paper route as a boy, I had to insert the Sunday funnies into the newspapers. I learned that if I made ten trips to the bathroom and was looking all around and talking about everything under the sun, it took me forever to get done. I had to be serious about my work if I wanted to get ahead. We need to learn that lesson in the Church.

Esau was not willing to suffer. Paul taught:

> *But in all things approving ourselves as the ministers of God, in much patience, in afflictions, in necessities, in distresses,*   2 Corinthians 6:4

> *Be not thou therefore ashamed of the testimony of our Lord, nor of me his prisoner: but be thou partaker of the afflictions of the gospel according to the power of God;*   2 Timothy 1:8

> *But thou hast fully known my doctrine, manner of life, purpose, faith, longsuffering, charity, patience, Persecutions, afflictions, which came unto me at Antioch, at Iconium, at Lystra; what persecutions I endured: but out of them all the Lord delivered me.*   2 Timothy 3:10-11

The psalmist agreed:

> *Many are the afflictions of the righteous: but the Lord delivereth him out of them all.*
>   Psalms 34:19

Some folks believe that once they get saved, life will be a "bed or roses." They have a lot of hard lessons to learn. Life can be even more difficult for a believer than for a nonbeliever. The difference is that we have Jesus to help us through every trial and test.

To be a great leader, you must have a sacrificial spirit. You must be willing to go the extra mile, to make even the ultimate sacrifice. If you are not, you will remain behind with the pack.

It is time that we stopped thinking only of our own little surroundings, our four walls, and nothing more. As long as we are concentrating only on our own needs and the things that will bring pleasure to us, we will never have a vision for the world, and will never be used of the Holy Ghost to bring revival.

The spirit of sacrifice is the spirit of Christ. He came to give. He taught us that it is better to give than to receive, and the more you give out, the more you get from God. Being withdrawn from the needs of others and thinking only of yourself leads to spiritual poverty. In politics, they are calling it "isolationism": *withdrawing from reality and the problems of the world, thinking only of ourselves.*

Such isolationism is evident in countries around the world, for man is essentially selfish and doesn't want to focus on the needs of others. Most people not willing to sacrifice personal comforts to help relieve the suffering of the world at large.

Jesus spoke of those who were unconcerned about the sheep as *"hirelings."* They would flee, He said, when danger presented itself, because they were thinking only of themselves and not of the welfare of the flock.

Many Christians have fallen into that category. They need the Holy Ghost to enlarge them, so that they will have a concern for the rest of the Body and will catch a vision of the needs of the world. They must become willing to think beyond themselves.

Some churches are so closed to the outside that they rarely invite speakers who are not of their particular denomination to come in. They have lost the vision of the Body and of the world. They are isolated within their own four walls and cannot see beyond themselves. This was Esau's sin and that which caused him to lose his place of inheritance. He did not want to give of himself.

If you are not ready to give of yourself, forget the gifts of the Spirit. They will operate in your life only when you have a genuine desire to be a blessing to somebody else. So, if you are only thinking about yourself, if you don't want to bless someone else, don't waste God's time seeking for those precious gifts.

If you are only thinking of your own comfort and convenience, you will never be in the right place at the right time to help anyone else anyway. But when you are unconcerned about self, and committed to blessing others, no sacrifice will be too great for you, and all nine of the gifts of the Spirit will flow forth from your life.

Jesus is our example. He learned obedience through suffering:

> *Though he were a Son, yet learned he obedience by the things which he suffered;*   Hebrews 5:8

Jesus was willing to lay down His life, to give Himself in sacrifice so that others might benefit. If we hope to be mightily used of God, we must learn to do the same.

The best way to grow is to give out to others. Sometimes you may feel exhausted, but if you will find someone in need and minister to them, God will strengthen you. We receive by giving.

When Esau refused to give out, he became like the Dead Sea. It is about 13 miles wide and 50 to 55 miles long. Seven bodies of water flow into it, the main one being the Jordan River. But, because it is situated at such a low spot, there is no way for the water to escape. It sits there and stagnates, becoming heavily saturated with minerals and incapable of supporting life. The Dead Sea is five times more salty than the Pacific Ocean; and nothing can live for long in its waters, because the water cannot move.

If you have no capacity to give out, you will lose your capacity to receive. When you are willing to give of yourself, God will multiply your efforts and make you fruitful.

The reason that Pentecost flourished in the early days of revival in America was because every church had people who dedicated themselves to intercession. There were prayer rooms that were frequently filled with people tarrying before the Lord. We have very few such sacrificial people today.

Some people are completely turned off by even the thought of sacrifice. Let's face facts. Working for God can have its moments of sacrifice. However, if God is moving and blessing in our lives and in our ministries, nothing else matters. No sacrifice is too great to see His blessing.

Some ministers who travel to other countries to preach, stay in the finest hotels. They are not happy, however, if they don't see the hand of God at work. Others who travel in ministry are willing to stay in the most humble surroundings. The surroundings don't matter, because they are experiencing the move of God's power in their lives.

Even our pastors have become unwilling to inconvenience themselves. Many of our churches let out early now, not because the people are unwilling to stay, but because the preacher himself wants to get home early. For the most part, when people are getting blessed, they don't want to go home early. If, on the other hand, there is no blessing, everyone wants to go home early.

Let us lay aside our feeble excuses and become willing to make whatever sacrifice is necessary to see the hand of God move upon the nations of the world in which we live.

Chapter 8

Why I Understand Esau

And such were some of you: but ye are washed, but ye are sanctified, but ye are justified in the name of the Lord Jesus, and by the Spirit of our God.
                                                                1 Corinthians 6:11

I think one of the reasons I have been so blessed through the years by the story of Jacob and Esau is that I understand Esau so well. I know exactly where he was coming from because I was just like him.

I was given to God by my parents to be a preacher even before I was born; but when I grew up, I didn't want to be a preacher. I had my sights on other things. I had other dreams. I had other plans in life. Being a preacher was the last thing I wanted to do with the rest of my life. I ran from God for twenty-nine years, primarily because I did not want to be in the ministry.

I had a godly father and mother, both of them in Christian ministry. My uncle was a preacher. Both my grandfather and grandmother on my mother's side were preachers. My sister was a preacher. But I was the blackest sinner that ever lived. I didn't want what they had. I ran in the opposite direction to avoid God.

I loved my dad, but I didn't want to get involved in any way with what he was doing. When I was in Richmond for a sales meeting, I would go to Ashland to see him. I always found my dad hard at work on the campground he loved so much; but I had no burden to help him. I visited and was gone — to do my own thing.

My parents often encouraged me, in my youth, to go with them to hear great preachers. They often traveled to hear William Branham, Jack Coe, Kathryn Kuhlman, and many others. I never went, and so I lost forever the opportunity to hear those great men and women of God. Traveling to another city just to hear a preacher sounded very boring to me. I had some more exciting and rewarding things to do. At least I thought they were more rewarding.

My father always did his best to interest me in the ministry. He introduced me to dozens of visiting ministers when I was younger. I never remembered their names and didn't care if I ever saw them again in this lifetime. I simply wasn't interested. I was glad when a young man began to work with my father so closely that Dad introduced him as his spiritual Timothy. I wasn't the least bit jealous. I was happy, thinking that his love for that young man took some of the pressure off of me to get into the spiritual activities. I had no interest whatsoever. If others wanted to do that, let them do it, but not me.

Like most everyone else, I knew that when I got old I would serve God. After all, that was the right thing to do. I did want to go to heaven; but there was plenty of time for all that later. I had to live first. For the present, I didn't want to identify with anything spiritual. Like Esau, I was selfish and could think of nothing but myself and my own personal happiness.

One of the reasons I didn't get saved for so long was that I resented the sacrifices my parents had made for the ministry. I saw them get up in the middle of the night and go out to pray for people who were sick. I saw them take the last money they had and use it to put gasoline in a car to send someone else out to preach — when our own family was in need. I saw God being put first and our family being put second, or third, or fourth. I heard my father say that we would pay the ministry bills before we would eat. My flesh couldn't agree with that thinking at all. I did not want to sacrifice, for any reason.

Like many others, I had never learned the joy that comes from giving of yourself to bless others. For too long we have had our hands extended to receive. It is time to give. The true joy of the Christian life is in giving. The spirit of Christ is the spirit of giving. He gave because He loved. I resisted these thoughts. I didn't want to give. I wanted to get all I could out of life.

Most of all, I didn't want God involved in my business. I was determined to be a success in life and to earn a good living. I didn't want Him to interfere with that. I was willing to pay my tithes because our parents had always taught us this was the way to prosper, but beyond the tithe, God had no part in my business.

When I attended the convention where I got saved, I heard people telling how God had been blessing them in business. As I listened to one after another of them tell how they had miraculously received an answer from God for their pressing business problems, I realized how foolish I had been to try to be successful by shutting God out of my business. I was ready to open my heart to Him and to allow Him to control my life entirely. I realized, nearly too late, how foolish I had been to want to avoid being spiritual, to avoid entering into the ministry, to avoid accepting the great spiritual heritage of our family. I was ready to obey God; and I have never been sorry.

I had always had the habit of attending church on Sunday morning, and I continued to attend — even when I had been in the bars on Saturday night. I wanted the services to be lively and the preachers to be anointed, even though I wasn't ready to live right myself. I hated it when the preacher would read from his notes. I hated it when he would take my hand at the back door and say, "Son, I hope you enjoyed the service; and I hope you will come back." I hated phonies. And I was the greatest of the phonies. Thank God he saved me from a life of mediocrity. Thank God He didn't reject my repentance, as He did Esau's. Thank God that I was able to find the joy of giving myself completely to God and His service.

Yes, I understand Esau perfectly and I don't want to be like him anymore. God is the most important thing in my life, and I am constantly struggling to be spiritual, to love God more than anything else and to walk in paths that please Him.

The lessons we learn from Esau are mostly negative ones; don't be an Esau.

On the other hand, there are a lot of positive things we can learn from Jacob and the experiences he had. In the following chapters, we will explore some of them.

Part III

Maintaining
the Birthright
and the Blessing

Chapter 9

Experience Your Own Bethel

And Jacob went out from Beersheba, and went to-
ward Haran. And he lighted upon a certain place,
and tarried there all night, because the sun was
set; and he took of the stones of that place, and put
them for his pillows, and lay down in that place
to sleep. Genesis 28:10-11

Jacob was forced to flee from home, from the mother he loved, from secure and familiar surroundings, and found himself in a strange place alone. The experience proved to be a good one for him, for he began crying out to God and had an unusual experience in a place he would call Bethel.

And he dreamed, and behold a ladder set up on the earth, and the top of it reached to heaven: and behold the angels of God ascending and descending on it.   Genesis 28:12

Night found Jacob in a deserted country place, and he was forced to sleep under the stars, using a stone for his pillow. And there he had a dream.

It is amazing how many dreams are recorded in the Bible. God thinks that dreams are important and longs to make us a people of dreams.

God spoke to Solomon in a dream soon after he assumed the throne:

In Gibeon the Lord appeared to Solomon in a dream by night: and God said, Ask what I shall give thee.   1 Kings 3:5

Through his dream, Solomon received wisdom to guide his people and was promised wealth and honor, as well.

We need to pay closer attention to our dreams. The Word of God declares:

I will bless the Lord, who hath given me counsel: my reins also instruct me in the night seasons.
                    Psalms 16:7

God wants to give us understanding, counsel and instruction, through dreams. It is a marvelous way to receive from God, because our bodies need rest, but our spirits don't need any rest. So, in the night, while our bodies are resting, God can speak to us just as well as He can during the day. Believe God to give you insight into the problems you face through spiritual dreams.

In his dream, Jacob saw the angels of the Lord ascending and descending a ladder, I believe that this shows us how our prayers are taken into the throne room of heaven. The Devil would try to stop your prayer from getting through, but there is a stairway, a channel, that neither the Devil nor the imps of Hell can block. When you and I get prayed through and get in the spirit, when we begin to pray according to the will of God, Jesus, who is seated at the right hand of the Father, is just waiting to make intercession for us. And the Devil cannot stop the prayer that we offer unto God.

This stairway is also the means by which a soul is escorted into the presence of God. Angels take that soul and ascend a stairway. Even in death, the Devil would like to steal the soul of the saints of God. But there is an armored guard, as it were, of the angelic forces of heaven on either side of that stairway standing guard, as other angels go up and down, taking the souls of those who have died in the Lord.

Stephen was one of those souls. He saw Jesus, as He stood with arms outstretched, to welcome him home.

But he, being full of the Holy Ghost, looked up stedfastly into heaven, and saw the glory of God, and Jesus standing on the right hand of God, And said, Behold, I see the heavens opened, and the Son of man standing on the right hand of God.
Acts 7:55-56

I believe that Jesus stands to welcome home every saint of God. As they draw their last breath of earth's atmosphere and begin to breathe heaven's glory, He says to them:

> *Well done, thou good and faithful servant: ... enter thou into the joy of thy lord.*   Matthew 25:21

This is the full meaning of Jacob's vision of the ladder. But more important than seeing angels, Jacob was seeing God. He was standing above the ladder, and He spoke to Jacob.

> *And, behold, the Lord stood above it, and said, I am the Lord God of Abraham thy father, and the God of Isaac: the land whereon thou liest, to thee will I give it, and to thy seed; And thy seed shall be as the dust of the earth, and thou shalt spread abroad to the west, and to the east, and to the north, and to the south: and in thee and in thy seed shall all the families of the earth be blessed. And, behold, I am with thee, and will keep thee in all places whither thou goest, and will bring thee again into this land; for I will not leave thee, until I have done that which I have spoken to thee of.*
> Genesis 28:13-15

It was good that Jacob saw God, because he needed God in that lonely hour. He had left home and did not know exactly where he was going or what would befall him there.

God identified Himself as *"the God of Abraham thy father, and the God of Isaac."* He was demonstrating that He wanted to be Jacob's God, as well. It must have thrilled Jacob to think, "He is not only the God of my grandfather, and the God of my father; but, thank God, He is my God too."

He can be your God today, for Jehovah has always been a personal God. He is a national God, and He is a family God, but His desire has always been to be a personal God.

He is not just a God of the past, of ancient history, He is the God of NOW, the God of today and today's situations. We don't have to fast and pray for a week to get His attention. He is seeking us long before we ever seek Him. He is calling us long before we ever get around to calling Him. He has promised:

> *And call upon me in the day of trouble: I will deliver thee, and thou shalt glorify me.*
> Psalms 50:15

All other thoughts had now vanished from Jacob's mind. He was in the presence of God; and that changed everything. He could never be the same from that moment.

As Jacob basked in the glory of God, God gave him many wonderful promises. He promised him the land he was lying on. He promised him, as He had to Abraham and Isaac before him, that his seed would be *"as the dust of the earth,"* and would spread abroad in every direction. He repeated to him the promise that all the families of the earth would be blessed because of him and his seed. He promised him that He would be with him everywhere he went. He promised Jacob that He would bring him back safely to his own land. He promised that He would never leave Jacob and that He would fulfill all of His commitments. Those are powerful promises that should give courage to every faint heart.

God will never fail to keep His promises. Paul said:

> *For what if some did not believe? shall their unbelief make the faith of God without effect? God forbid: yea, let God be true, but every man a liar;*
> Romans 3:3-4

When God has given you a promise, in any form, you can stand on it. No detail of it will fail. The angel Gabriel said to Mary:

> *And blessed is she that believed: for there shall be a performance of those things which were told her from the Lord.*   Luke 1:45

If you believe, you will always see the performance of the things you are believing for. God never fails. His Word is sure.

I don't know about you, but God has given me some wonderful promises. There are many unfulfilled prophecies over my life. I am not forgetting them, and I am not letting God forget them. I remind myself often, and I remind Him. His promise is that every word will be fulfilled.

When I contracted typhoid fever in Pakistan in 1968 and nearly died, the promise of God kept me going. My body was lifeless from the waist down. I was so hot that a vapor, much like steam, was rising from my body. I was unable to walk more than a few feet at a time. But I remembered a prophecy my mother had given over me before I left home. "Thou shalt go and return," I remembered her saying. So, I knew that I could not die somewhere along the way. I knew that I would get back home — because God said: *Thou shalt go and return.*

That seemed like a very simple part of the prophecy. Some might even consider it immaterial or unimportant; but those words saved my life. I clung to that promise of God when I could do nothing else, and God got me home.

You don't need an encyclopedia-sized prophecy from God. Just a few words will suffice sometimes.

Heaven and earth shall pass away, but my words shall not pass away. Matthew 24:35

If God has spoken to you, don't let the Devil shake your faith. When everything seems to be impossible, say, "God, you are the God of the impossible, and You are the One who has spoken. I trust You now to bring it to pass." And He will do it.

We can say, as Moses to the children of Israel:

I call heaven and earth to witness ... this day ... .
Deuteronomy 4:26

The promises of God put the assets of Heaven at our disposal. Hallelujah!

All of this happened to Jacob while he was sleeping. Sleep can be a wonderful time. We take it too much for granted and usually don't expect God to do great things while we are sleeping. But He wants to.

When Jacob awoke, he knew that he had been in the presence of God. He said, *"Surely the Lord is in this place; and I knew it not."*

> *And Jacob awaked out of his sleep, and he said,*
> *Surely the Lord is in this place; and I knew it not.*
> *And he was afraid, and said, How dreadful is this*
> *place! this is none other but the house of God, and*
> *this is the gate of heaven.* Genesis 28:16-17

When he had first lain down on that hard earth with that rock under his head, Jacob may have been thinking about home. He may have been contemplating what kind of woman he would find among his mother's people to be his wife. He may have been thinking about Mama's biscuits. Or he may have been thinking about how much he missed his nice, warm bed.

When he woke up, however, Jacob had forgotten everything else. All thought of self was gone. "God is here!" What else is there to think about? He forgot that he was running for his life. He forgot that things hadn't worked out as he and his mother had planned. He forgot that he was on a trip to a strange place. He forgot about the wife he was seeking. He forgot about

how hard that rock pillow had been. "God is here!"
What else could possibly be important?

David said:

*In thy presence is fulness of joy; at thy right hand
there are pleasures for evermore.*   Psalms 16:11

We don't appreciate God enough. We don't appreciate His presence enough. We don't appreciate His
voice enough. We don't appreciate His provision
enough. We don't appreciate His servants enough. We
don't appreciate His Church enough.

When we are totally taken with the presence of God,
nothing else matters. It is only when we are not seeing
God work in our lives that we become consumed with
material things. When God is moving, natural things
lose their glamour.

Jacob was so overcome by his experience that, instead of ranting against the hard rock he had used as a
pillow and his lack of proper rest, because of not being
at home in his own comfortable bed, he took that hard
thing and made it into an altar to God. He took some
oil and poured it on top of that hard rock, and it became a sacred spot.

*And Jacob rose up early in the morning, and took
the stone that he had put for his pillows, and set it
up for a pillar, and poured oil upon the top of it.
And he called the name of that place Bethel: but
the name of that city was called Luz at the first.*
Genesis 28:18-19

The anointing can make all the difference in your life. It can turn hard things into blessed things. That which seems to be hard will turn out to be the greatest thing that ever happened to you in all of your life. Later, you can look back and say, "The things we went through in that place were difficult. They stretched us beyond measure. But the victories we gained are wonderful."

The hard places in our lives reveal the true nature of our experience. If everything comes easily, anyone could do it. It is the challenges in life that prove what we are made of. Don't be afraid of the hard places. Turn them into victories by meeting God in the midst of every crisis.

Anybody can shout when everyone else is shouting. Anyone can be happy when everyone else is happy. Everybody can run and dance when everybody else is running and dancing. When everybody else stops shouting, and you can keep on shouting, that's a sign you have a special touch from God.

Jacob was so changed by his experience that we could say that he was no longer the same man. One man lay down, but a different man got up. The natural man lay down, and a spiritual man got up. A man who had little of God was now a man who knew that God had a great plan for his life.

The Devil doesn't want you to know that God has a great plan for your life. He doesn't want you to know that God needs you. Our need is mutual: we need God, and He needs us. He could have used angels to perform His work, but He chose us.

He is not about to send someone from another plane to do His work. He sends us.

Jacob called the place he had met God Bethel. *Beth* is the Hebrew word meaning *house*, and *El* is the Hebrew word for *God*. *Bethel*, therefore, literally means *the house of God*, just as Jacob said. When he spoke of *the house of God* and *the gate of Heaven*, he wasn't referring to some man-made structure, because he was out in the open air, away from buildings. But there, in that open place, he had a personal encounter with God.

God can meet you anywhere. He will meet you as you are riding down the road in your automobile. He will meet you on your hospital bed. He will meet you in your prison cell. He will meet you on your job. He is where you need Him to be.

He will meet you in the cornfield. He will meet you in the kitchen. He will meet you in the bedroom. You can have your Bethel wherever you are.

Nothing can replace an intimate relationship with the Lord. In marriage, it is necessary for a husband and wife to share both the joys and the heartaches of marital life without allowing anything to come between them and spoil their special relationship. They can never turn their attention to a third party.

This is the secret of power with God, as well. He is longing for an intimate relationship with His people. He wants you to commit to giving Him all your attention and speaking with Him at your own personal Bethel.

The story is told of a couple who had been married many years. They were driving somewhere in the car and the wife was nagging her husband. "I don't understand why you don't treat me like you used to. Just look at us now. When we were young, you loved to put your arm around me and hold me tight. You never do that anymore."

The husband looked down at the large space between them and answered, "I ain't moved."

As far as he was concerned it was the wife's fault. She used to sit closer to him, which made it easy for him to embrace her. He was sitting in the same place; she was the one who had moved.

In the same way, God hasn't changed. He hasn't moved. He is still waiting on us to come near. He is ever ready and eager to embrace us.

Sometimes we wonder why God is not hearing our prayer. In those moments we need to draw a little closer to Him. He promised:

> *Draw nigh to God, and he will draw nigh to you.*
> James 4:8

If you want more blessings, move higher in God. There are different anointings and different blessings on every spiritual level in God. If you need more, move higher, come closer.

Everyone wants to get the blessings without getting the God of blessings, but the two go together. God goes with blessings, and Satan goes with cursings. Come to Bethel and be blessed.

702.94
783
148 59 94
17 35
146859
(310
1158 59

Chapter 10

Don't Be Afraid To Make A Vow To God

And Jacob vowed a vow, saying, If God will be with me, and will keep me in this way that I go, and will give me bread to eat, and raiment to put on, So that I come again to my father's house in peace; then shall the Lord be my God: And this stone, which I have set for a pillar, shall be God's house: and of all that thou shalt give me I will surely give the tenth unto thee.

Genesis 28:20-22

The things that Jacob was expecting God to do for him are the very things God had already said He would do. Jacob, therefore, had a right to expect them and a right to remind God of them.

I remind God sometimes. "Remember, Lord, You said: *'If ye abide in me, and my words abide in you, ye shall ask what ye will, and it shall be done unto you'* (John 15:7)." He doesn't mind my doing that.

"God, You said, in John 14, verses 12 and 13: *'Verily, verily, I say unto you, He that believeth on me, the works that I do shall he do also; and greater works than these shall he do; because I go unto my Father. And whatsoever ye shall ask in my name, that will I do, that the Father may be glorified in the Son.'* I am expecting to do the same works that You did because of that promise."

Jacob was doing that same thing. God told him that He would never leave him. So, Jacob responded, "If You are going to be my God, and You are going to take care of me, and You are going to put raiment on my back and give me food to eat and will bring me again back unto this land ... ," etc.

God had told Jacob some impossible things that night. He wasn't even married yet, and God said his descendants would be as the dust of the earth. Those were amazing words to a bachelor, but God knew what He was talking about. Over the next twenty years, Jacob would have twelve sons and a daughter.

Jacob believed what God was saying and repeated it: "God, since You are going to be with me, and since You are going to put clothes on my back and food on my table and will bring me safely back unto this land and back unto my father's house, I am going to serve

You, and I am going to give you one tenth of all that You bless me with."

When Jacob made that vow to God, a new chapter began in his life. He was not blessed through deceit and lies; he was blessed through a personal commitment to God. And, even though he went out empty, unable to carry more than the small lunch his mother, no doubt, prepared for him to eat along the way, when he returned to Bethel, twenty years later, he came back full.

Jacob returned a generous man. When he met his brother, Esau, after so many years, he insisted on giving him many gifts. Esau said he didn't need it, but Jacob insisted. He had learned to be generous and that you can never lose by being generous.

Esau said, "I've got enough."

And Jacob said, "I've been blessed so much by God, I just want you to take it. Just take it. I have so much." And he kept insisting until Esau agreed to take the gifts he offered.

Jacob left home with nothing, but after he decided to walk with God and to enter into a covenant with Him, he came back full. When Jacob made a vow to God and kept it, he was blessed.

I believe we can make that same covenant with God, and I believe we can be blessed like Jacob. If God keeps His promises to us, why should we be afraid to keep our promises to Him? We cannot lose by obeying God. We can only prosper.

God has promised to be with us, just as He promised He would be with Jacob.

Lo, I am with you alway, even unto the end of the world. Amen.   Matthew 28:20

I will never leave thee, nor forsake thee.
                                        Hebrews 13:5

God has promised to supply our needs, just as He promised to supply Jacob's needs.

But my God shall supply all your need according to his riches in glory by Christ Jesus.
                                        Philippians 4:19

God has promised to protect us, just as He promised to protect Jacob.

O my God ... thou hast smitten all mine enemies upon the cheek bone; thou hast broken the teeth of the ungodly.   Psalms 3:7

Out of the mouth of babes and sucklings hast thou ordained strength because of thine enemies, that thou mightest still the enemy and the avenger.
                                        Psalms 8:2

We have a great inheritance awaiting us, just as Jacob did.

And now, brethren, I commend you to God, and to the word of his grace, which is able to build you up, and to give you an inheritance among all them which are sanctified.   Acts 20:32

> *To open their eyes, and to turn them from dark-*
> *ness to light, and from the power of Satan unto*
> *God, that they may receive forgiveness of sins, and*
> *inheritance among them which are sanctified by*
> *faith that is in me.* Acts 26:18

After he had met God face to face, Jacob was not afraid to make a covenant with Him. He was sure that he could lose nothing. There wasn't much that Jacob could do physically for God, but he could give a token of his appreciation, a recognition that everything belongs to the Creator of the Universe. The tithe, then, became his firstfruits offering, a symbol of his covenant with God.

Ten per cent of what we earn isn't much, but it is very important to give it. It means the difference between poverty and prosperity, between just getting by and having an abundance.

By tithing on our earnings, we are not trying to buy God's favor. No amount of money could do that. What price could we put on the many blessings God has given us through the years? Even one of His blessings is beyond price. Tithing is a sign of our faithfulness to the covenant we have made with God.

When we are faithful with our part, God never fails with His. He manifests His presence on our behalf. He puts food on our tables; He puts clothes on our backs; He protects us from harm; and He loads us with daily benefits.

Jacob came back full, despite every obstacle he encountered in the way. God is not limited by circumstances. He never fails — regardless of the circumstances.

God is ready to fulfill all His promises to us, but there is a level of commitment necessary on our part for their fulfillment. When the Holy Ghost speaks in prophecy and you toss that prophetic word over your shoulder and don't want to receive it, God is not obligated to fulfill it for you. If, on the other hand, you reach out and grab it and say, "I take that; that's for me; that's mine; God is speaking to me," then God will move Heaven and Earth to bring to pass the word He has given you.

You and I can stand upon the promise that God has made and can watch, as God moves by His mighty power to bring to pass His plan and His promise for each of us.

The covenant that Jacob made with God didn't signify sacrifice on his part; it signified the provision of God for his life; it signified the protection of God over his life; it signified God's favor upon him. That made it worth every effort. Jacob could not lose by entering into a pact with God. He could only gain.

And God doesn't have to do the same thing every time. He wants to speak to us in some new ways, to reveal Himself in some new ways. Don't expect Him to always move in the same way and speak in the same way. He is a God of variety.

Now unto him that is able to do exceeding abundantly above all that we ask or think, according to the power that worketh in us,   Ephesians 3:20

God is a God of covenant. He has always covenanted with man. And He has never failed to keep His covenant. A covenant is a contract, a bargain, if you will. And God always keeps His part of the bargain. However, a bargain, a contract, requires the action of two parties. God keeps His part, when we keep our part. When we fail to hold up our end of the bargain, God is released from His obligation.

Jacob entered into a financial arrangement with God. He had nothing to lose. He had come away from home with nothing. So, he had nothing to lose. Some people are so afraid they are going to lose something by giving to God, and they end up robbing themselves of the many blessings they could have.

Jacob made a vow to God, and he kept that vow. Then, when he returned home after twenty years of living abroad, he was so wealthy that he was looking for ways to give things away.

Say YES to God: Yes, I will make a vow. Yes, I will make a pledge. Yes, I will help clean the church. Yes, I will house the visitors. Yes, I will participate in the labor of the church. Yes, I will support the ministry with my financial giving.

Say it, if you mean to do it. On the other hand, let me warn you that it is a dangerous thing to make a vow to God and not keep that vow. If you don't intend to keep your agreement, it is better not to vow.

Better is it that thou shouldest not vow, than that thou shouldest vow and not pay.

Ecclesiastes 5:5

If you don't plan to do what you are saying to God, don't let your mouth make the commitment. Don't let your mouth get you into trouble. It is better not to promise than to promise and never fulfill.

Poor people are usually more faithful in paying their tithes than those who have more funds available. I believe there are two reasons for that fact. First, what the poor are giving is not very much. As our income increases and we have more to give, ten percent seems like a lot to give — although it still represents the same portion of our earnings. The percentage of those who tithe faithfully decreases proportionally with the amount of money people earn.

The second reason is that the poor realize they need God's blessings on their finances. Those who have prospered often feel that they no longer require God's help.

The same is true of time. People who have lesser abilities have less of a problem in giving God time. Those who can demand a larger hourly rate for their time feel that their time is too important to give to God.

When I give God the first hour of the day, I find that the rest of the day always goes more smoothly. If we feel that we don't have time to wait before the Lord, we are on our own, and things don't go as well for us.

The problem with Jacob's giving is that we don't know to WHOM he gave. Most of us like to give to God because He is perfect. But, because no church or minister is perfect, we use that as an excuse not to give.

It is true; there are no perfect churches. There are problems in all churches, and if you look for them, you will find them. But you cannot wait until you find a perfect church to start paying tithes and supporting the church. You must do it now — if you want God's blessing.

When I got saved, I made a pledge of $250, to be paid at $20 a month. After I had sent in my first two payments of $20, I noted that the organization changed directions and stopped doing the things they were doing when I made my commitment. I thought that was justification for not continuing my support. After all, "They are not doing what they were doing before." That thinking seemed very logical to me.

But the next time I got up to challenge other people to pay their vows, the Lord said to me, "What about your vow?"

"But, Lord," I protested, "I didn't pay my vow because they changed. And I don't agree with the new direction they are taking."

Once I had made my argument, I was sure that would be the end of the matter. I was convinced that I had done the right thing. But every time I got up to challenge other people in their giving, God reminded me of my own failure.

My reasoning was a convenient excuse. The truth is that I didn't have much money. Only recently saved, I was learning to live by faith. Two hundred and ten dollars was like two thousand dollars to me. It was hard for me to pay, and I jumped at the chance to get out of my commitment when the organization changed direction.

But God didn't accept my excuse. When I continued to repeat the same excuse, God said to me, "It doesn't matter what they have done. You didn't make your vow to them. You made it to ME."

Finally, I said, "God, if you will put the money in my hand, I will pay it." Very quickly the Lord placed that money in my hand. I paid my pledge and was blessed because of it.

Stop looking for every reason not to do what God has spoken to you to do and what you have vowed to do. Start looking for reasons to do what God requires of you and to fulfil your commitments. Then you will see the blessings of heaven.

What should a married woman do in the case that her husband won't allow her to tithe? If that is the case, she can't tithe for him, on what he receives; but she can be faithful with the money she receives or money that he gives her to run the household. Each of us must find some way to obey God.

In the case of the married woman who has an unbelieving husband, the Scriptures teach us that a sanctified wife sanctifies the husband. You do the right thing, and that will bring your husband to God.

> *For the unbelieving husband is sanctified by the wife, and the unbelieving wife is sanctified by the husband: else were your children unclean; but now are they holy.*   1 Corinthians 7:14

If you only get $10, you owe God $1. He knows your situation. You are only accountable for what passes through your hands. God will do the impossible for you — if you are faithful to your commitments.

Fifty years ago, some members of my father's church gave him $30 to buy a new suit. They knew that he was a stickler for paying his tithes. And they knew that if he paid his tithes on that $30 gift, he would not have enough for the new suit, because it cost exactly $30. So they gave him another gift of $3.00 to pay his tithes. When they got to thinking about it, they knew that my father would have to pay tithes on the $3.00, so they included another thirty cents in the gift. Being sure that he would want to pay tithes on the thirty cents, they included another three cents to enable him to do so and still get the $30 suit. That's how careful my father was about paying tithes.

If you are exact with God, He will be exact with you. He will give to you with the same measure you give to Him. One man that my parents knew deducted the wear on his shoe leather from his paycheck before figuring his tithes. By doing that, he was only robbing himself. You can't afford to be miserly with God. Give to Him liberally, and you will receive in the same measure.

God loves a hilarious (cheerful) giver.

Every man according as he purposeth in his heart, so let him give; not grudgingly, or of necessity: for God loveth a cheerful giver.   2 Corinthians 9:7

If you have made a vow to God, be faithful in paying it. It may not relate to finances. Whatever it is, keep it; and God will bless you for it.

We are not the owners of the things that are in our pockets and pocketbooks and in our houses. We are only stewards of the things which God has entrusted to us. If we can learn that lesson, if we can hear the voice of God and be obedient in that which He has entrusted to our care, we will have full pockets and full pocketbooks and full houses; for God never forgets. His memory is unfailing.

The key to financial prosperity is having the correct motivation. It is not wrong to want to have full pockets and full houses and full bank accounts. God wants to fill them for us, but the motivation must be holy. The purpose of God filling our need is so that we can minister to the needs of others. If we miss that, we are missing the most important thing in life.

Turn that hand over. Don't just use it to get, use it to give.

Paul wrote a whole chapter in his letter to the Corinthians to show us that it is possible to have all nine of the gifts of the Spirit and to still be like *"sounding brass"* and *"tinkling cymbals."* Proper motivation, God's love toward all mankind, makes all the difference.

But when the spirit of giving comes upon us, and we are willing to say, "Holy Ghost, give me a double portion that I might bless others. Anoint my hands that I may minister healing to those who are sick," then the Lord will bless us and bless us and bless us and bless us some more.

Because our heavenly Father has our greatest welfare at heart, don't be afraid to make a vow to God.

Chapter 11

Claim What Is Rightfully Yours

*Then Jacob went on his journey, and came into the
land of the people of the east.*   Genesis 29:1

After his experience at Bethel, Jacob went on his way
to find the bride God had prepared for him. He traveled to the land of his mother's people. As he traveled
he came upon a small group of men gathered about a
common well.

> *And he looked, and behold a well in the field, and,
> lo, there were three flocks of sheep lying by it; for*

> *out of that well they watered the flocks: and a great*
> *stone was upon the well's mouth. And thither*
> *were all the flocks gathered: and they rolled the*
> *stone from the well's mouth, and watered the*
> *sheep, and put the stone again upon the well's*
> *mouth in his place.*   Genesis 2-3

The village well, in those days, was one of the most important assets of the village and was the focal point of much activity. The women often gathered there to wash clothes or to draw water for drinking and cooking in the house. At other times, the flocks were brought for watering. Jacob arrived just at the watering time. Isn't the timing of the Lord a wonderful thing! I only wish more of us could be more keen in the Spirit about His timing.

This particular well was never left unprotected. When it was not being used, it was covered with a great stone to protect it from dust and falling debris and to discourage enemies from fouling or filling in the well. When all the women were ready to draw their household water, the covering stone was taken off. Or when all the flocks were gathered and waiting nearby, the cover would be removed and the precious water would be drawn.

Water is important. No human can live without it. No animal can live without it. No plant can live without it. Water is life-giving. Water is life-sustaining. We can't exist without it.

When Jacob came upon the small group of men, he stopped to ask them if they knew Laban, his mother's brother. They told him they did and that, even then, Laban's daughter was approaching with the flocks of her father.

> *And Jacob said unto them, My brethren, whence be ye? And they said, Of Haran are we. And he said unto them, Know ye Laban the son of Nahor? And they said, We know him. And he said unto them, Is he well? And they said, He is well: and, behold, Rachel his daughter cometh with the sheep. And he said, Lo, it is yet high day, neither is it time that the cattle should be gathered together: water ye the sheep, and go and feed them.*
> *And they said, We cannot, until all the flocks be gathered together, and till they roll the stone from the well's mouth; then we water the sheep.*
> Genesis 29:4-8

When Jacob lifted up his eyes and beheld the young Rachel approaching, his heart leaped for joy. It was love at first sight. He knew this was the woman of his dreams.

> *And while he yet spake with them, Rachel came with her father's sheep; for she kept them.*
> Genesis 29:9

In the land of Rebekah, women were important and had important jobs. Flocks were valuable and were not entrusted to just anyone. When Moses met his wife, Jethro's daughter, she was also taking care of the sheep. Caring for the flocks was a hard job for anyone. Yet, it was entrusted to women. Women make fine workers. Don't limit them, pastors.

Rachel was probably not elaborately dressed or adorned. Sheep herders don't dress up for their work. But that didn't matter to Jacob. He knew that this was his intended wife.

The cover of the well was so heavy that it took several men to remove it. Since three flocks of sheep had already gathered, there must have been at least three men already there. Yet they told Jacob that they were not able to remove the stone. When Jacob saw Rachel, he was so excited that he removed the huge stone single-handedly.

> *And it came to pass, when Jacob saw Rachel the daughter of Laban his mother's brother, and the sheep of Laban his mother's brother, that Jacob went near, and rolled the stone from the well's mouth, and watered the flock of Laban his mother's brother.*   Genesis 29:10

The girl was lovely, a feast for Jacob's eyes. As he watched her, he was even more sure now of God's will for him. He ran to her and kissed her. The Scriptures say:

> *And Jacob kissed Rachel, and lifted up his voice, and wept.*   Genesis 29:11

What a touching scene!

It is not without importance that the two met at the well. When Eliezer, the servant of Abraham, had been sent to find a wife for Isaac (the wife he found was Rebekah), he had found her at the well, under very similar circumstances. Jacob's mother was discovered in the same way he was now discovering his own wife. No doubt he had heard the story of Eliezer and the well many times through his childhood and youth. So, it was very significant for him to find Rachel at the well.

At the well, we can find a lot of good things from God.

Eliezer was a type of the Holy Ghost, sent by Abraham, a type of the Father, to get a bride for Isaac, a type of the Son. He was looking for a woman who would give him water to drink, a woman who had life to offer. Rebekah was that woman. She also offered to water his camels.

Camels have an enormous water capacity. One camel can drink many gallons of water at a time. Then, camels can travel for days overland without water because they drink so much at one time and store it. There was no pump on that well, and Rebekah had to draw enough water for all those camels by hand. That was very hard work.

Eliezer was so excited when he learned that Rebekah was from the right family. She was *"fair to look upon,"* she was a virgin, and she was willing to work. This was the answer to his prayers, and these are characteristics of the Bride of Christ. God is looking for willing workers who can make up His Bride.

It is not enough to be filled with the Spirit, we must put our gifts to work for God. Only about 10% of the members of the church make any effort to do anything for God. He is looking for willing workers.

> *Whatsoever thy hand findeth to do, do it with thy might; for there is no work, nor device, nor knowledge, nor wisdom, in the grave, whither thou goest.*   Ecclesiastes 9:10

Rebekah was excited as she ran home because Eliezer (the type of the Holy Ghost), had given her gifts. And the Holy Ghost gives us gifts before the wedding. These gifts are only a foretaste of the glory that awaits us in heaven, after the wedding takes place.

When her brother, Laban, learned that a stranger had come to town and that he was bearing gifts, he could not resist running to meet the man. He insisted that Eliezer come to their home and stay with them. Some things don't seem to ever change.

> *And Jacob told Rachel that he was her father's brother, and that he was Rebekah's son: and she ran and told her father. And it came to pass, when Laban heard the tidings of Jacob his sister's son, that he ran to meet him, and embraced him, and brought him to his house. And he told Laban all these things.*   Genesis 29:12-13

When Rachel ran home to tell her father, the very same Laban, about this unusual man who had come, the one who had been able to move the stone from the well all by himself and who had been so happy to see her and had kissed her, Laban was delighted with the news.

Laban was a very enterprising and fairly devious man. That a stranger had come to town was very interesting to him. He wanted to meet this man, who turned out to be his own sister's child.

He ran excitedly to greet Jacob in the way, kissing him in greeting and welcoming him into his own house, just as he had done with Eliezer so many years before. When they had sat down together, Jacob explained the circumstances of his coming and Laban insisted that he stay.

> *And Laban said to him, Surely thou art my bone and my flesh. And he abode with him the space of a month.*   Genesis 29:14

Laban was a flatterer, who would take advantage of his nephew many times over the coming years. By the time that first month had passed Laban was fairly sure what the intentions of Jacob were. He was positive that Jacob was obsessed with the lovely apparition he had first seen at the well, and was also sure that he could make a good deal for the hand of his daughter.

He approached Jacob and said that he felt it was unfair not to pay him for the valuable work he was doing among the flocks, although he was a relative and was enjoying the hospitality of their home. He told Jacob to name his own price. Just as he had been sure his nephew would do, Jacob offered to work without wages, but for the right to the hand of Rachel in marriage and, without bargaining, offered seven full years of service for the privilege.

> *And Jacob loved Rachel; and said, I will serve thee seven years for Rachel thy younger daughter.*
>
> Genesis 29:18

Laban was delighted, and the deal was struck without further haggling.

How long those seven years must have been for a man who had been a bachelor so long and was so in love! Surprisingly, however, that period is summarized in just one Bible verse:

> *And Jacob served seven years for Rachel; and they seemed unto him but a few days, for the love he had to her.*
>
> Genesis 29:20

Isn't love an amazing thing! And wouldn't it be wonderful if we could all love the Lord with that same fervor as Jacob loved Rachel!

Jacob worked hard for seven years. But, when the seven years had passed, he was ready to get his wife.

> *And Jacob said unto Laban, Give me my wife, for my days are fulfilled.*
>
> Genesis 29:21

What happened next is one of the most unusual stories in the Bible. Laban prepared a wedding feast and invited all his neighbors to attend. The proper ceremonies were performed; and, at the appointed time, Laban led his daughter to Jacob's tent, leaving the two alone to pass the night in matrimonial bliss.

When Jacob awoke in the morning, he was horrified to find himself looking into the face of Leah, Rachel's older sister. It was the first time he had discovered the switch. Either Leah said nothing all night long or she disguised her voice.

What a humiliating circumstance! What could he do? He ran to Laban and demanded to know why he had been defrauded after he had served faithfully for seven years.

> *And it came to pass, that in the morning, behold, it was Leah: and he said to Laban, What is this thou hast done unto me? did not I serve with thee for Rachel? wherefore then hast thou beguiled me?*
> Genesis 29:25

Laban's answer was that he was just following the custom of his people. His people never gave a daughter in marriage while an older one remained single. Isn't it strange that he didn't tell Jacob about this custom seven years earlier? Had he just learned the custom? Was this really the custom? There is no way of knowing. What we do know is that Jacob didn't get the woman he loved and got another woman that he hadn't bargained for.

Probably Laban knew from the beginning exactly what he would do at the end of the seven years. He saw before him a moonstruck bachelor who could be easily taken advantage of, and he had pulled it off very nicely. Jacob had been willing to do whatever was necessary to get Rachel, and Laban knew it.

Seeing Jacob's anguish, Laban decided to take advantage of the moment. "I feel very sorry about what has happened," he must have said. "It is lamentable that you didn't understand our customs. This must be terrible for you. I know that you love Rachel. I'll tell you what I'll do. If you are willing to work for me another seven years, I will give you Rachel too. And I will not make you wait for her until the seven years are accomplished. You are a man of honor. I will give her to you now. What do you say?"

"But, I will have to ask of you two things in return for my kindness. First, don't make a public fuss about all of this. Many guests have come for this seven-day celebration. The festivities are just beginning. Don't spoil it for us by making an ugly scene. And, secondly, give Leah the seven days of uninterrupted honeymoon she deserves. Make it memorable for her. Then, at the end of the seven days, when the guests have gone home, I will give you Rachel."

What could Jacob say? His father-in-law had him at a definite disadvantage.

For so many years Jacob had lived alone. For seven years he had labored for one woman. Now, within the space of seven days, he had two women to contend with.

Old Eastern law permitted a man to have four wives — if he could take care of them. I once asked one of our

Egyptian guides what he thought about that law. "We have learned a hard lesson," he answered, "that having four wives means having four times as many problems."

Jacob had two, and they were sisters. It is hard to imagine the jealousy that existed between them from the very first day. Jacob's only consolation was that he had the woman he loved.

During the next seven years, Jacob served his father-in-law, tried to keep his squabbling wives happy, and sired eleven of the twelve boys who would form the backbone of the future tribes of Israel.

When his time of service was ended, Jacob told his uncle that it was time for him to move on.

> *And it came to pass, when Rachel had born Joseph, that Jacob said unto Laban, Send me away, that I may go unto mine own place, and to my country. Give me my wives and my children, for whom I have served thee, and let me go: for thou knowest my service which I have done thee.*
> Genesis 30:25-26

Laban was not happy with the prospect of losing such a good worker. He realized that he had been blessed by Jacob's presence, and he made him a business proposal that he hoped he could not refuse.

> *And Laban said unto him, I pray thee, if I have found favour in thine eyes, tarry: for I have learned by experience that the Lord hath blessed*

> *me for thy sake. And he said, Appoint me thy*
> *wages, and I will give it.*   Genesis 30:27-28

This time Jacob sensed that he had the advantage. He reminded Laban of the condition of his herds before he had begun caring for them and suggested a way in which he might have his fair share of them.

> *And he said unto him, Thou knowest how I have*
> *served thee, and how thy cattle was with me. For it*
> *was little which thou hadst before I came, and it is*
> *now increased unto a multitude; and the Lord*
> *hath blessed thee since my coming: and now when*
> *shall I provide for mine own house also?*
> *And he said, What shall I give thee?*
> *And Jacob said, Thou shalt not give me any thing:*
> *if thou wilt do this thing for me, I will again feed*
> *and keep thy flock. I will pass through all thy flock*
> *to day, removing from thence all the speckled and*
> *spotted cattle, and all the brown cattle among the*
> *sheep, and the spotted and speckled among the*
> *goats: and of such shall be my hire. So shall my*
> *righteousness answer for me in time to come,*
> *when it shall come for my hire before thy face:*
> *every one that is not speckled and spotted among*
> *the goats, and brown among the sheep, that shall*
> *be counted stolen with me.*
> *And Laban said, Behold, I would it might be ac-*
> *cording to thy word.*   Genesis 30:29-34

These were two deal makers, and an acceptable agreement was quickly reached. Jacob would continue tending the herds of Laban; but, from that day forward, calves and kids and lambs born speckled or spotted would belong to Jacob. The rest would belong to Laban. Both parties seemed to be satisfied with the deal.

No sooner had the conversation ended, however, than Laban called his sons and told them to remove all speckled and spotted cattle and goats and sheep from the herds and to move them to another location, three days journey away. He knew a good thing when he had it and was ready to do everything in his power to prevent Jacob from leaving. Surely this would prevent the birth of animals fitting the description Jacob had given.

And he removed that day the he goats that were ringstraked and spotted, and all the she goats that were speckled and spotted, and every one that had some white in it, and all the brown among the sheep, and gave them into the hand of his sons.
Genesis 30:35

But Jacob was not defeated. He could have been defeated after being humiliated into accepting the wrong wife. He could have been defeated after working fourteen years and having nothing to show for it in assets for his own family. He could have been defeated by being cheated again now. But he wasn't. He could not forget the words God had spoken at Bethel, and they kept his spirits high. He was not destined for defeat. He was destined for greatness.

He was sure that God had given him the word about the speckled and spotted animals, so he decided to take things into his own hands, in an elaborate scheme to make the strong among the existing animals produce speckled and spotted offspring, which would belong to him.

> *And Jacob took him rods of green poplar, and of the hazel and chesnut tree; and pilled white strakes in them, and made the white appear which was in the rods. And he set the rods which he had pilled before the flocks in the gutters in the watering troughs when the flocks came to drink, that they should conceive when they came to drink. And the flocks conceived before the rods, and brought forth cattle ringstraked, speckled, and spotted. And Jacob did separate the lambs, and set the faces of the flocks toward the ringstraked, and all the brown in the flock of Laban; and he put his own flocks by themselves, and put them not unto Laban's cattle. And it came to pass, whensoever the stronger cattle did conceive, that Jacob laid the rods before the eyes of the cattle in the gutters, that they might conceive among the rods. But when the cattle were feeble, he put them not in: so the feebler were Laban's, and the stronger Jacob's.* Genesis 30:37-42

Amazingly enough, this farfetched scheme actually seemed to work. It seems to have been a prophetic act, showing Jacob's great faith in God.

*And the man increased exceedingly, and had much
cattle, and maidservants, and menservants, and
camels, and asses.*   Genesis 30:43

Was it Jacob's scheme that changed the makeup of
the newborn animals, or what was it?

This apparent miracle infuriated Laban's sons. They
accused Jacob of cheating their father, and Laban,
seeing what was happening, turned against him, too.

*And he heard the words of Laban's sons, saying,
Jacob hath taken away all that was our father's;
and of that which was our father's hath he gotten
all this glory. And Jacob beheld the countenance of
Laban, and, behold, it was not toward him as
before.*   Genesis 31:1-2

When this happened, the Lord told Jacob that it was
now time to leave and return to his own land.

*And the Lord said unto Jacob, Return unto the
land of thy fathers, and to thy kindred; and I will
be with thee.*   Genesis 31:3

Jacob called his family together and told them what
God had said. He also revealed to them the mystery of
how they had become so wealthy in a short time. He
said that God had shown him how HE had taken cattle
away from Laban and given them to Jacob. An angel
spoke to him in a dream and showed him how God
had done it.

*And it came to pass at the time that the cattle
conceived, that I lifted up mine eyes, and saw in a
dream, and, behold, the rams which leaped upon
the cattle were ringstraked, speckled, and grisled.
And the angel of God spake unto me in a dream,
saying, Jacob: And I said, Here am I. And he said,
Lift up now thine eyes, and see, all the rams which
leap upon the cattle are ringstraked, speckled, and
grisled: for I have seen all that Laban doeth
unto thee.*   Genesis 31:10-12

Jacob had tried to change nature by putting rods
before the animals as they ate and drank, believing
that this would affect their conception. This, of course,
is not what really happened, but God saw his faith. I
believe that whatever he did would have worked. God
had his hand in the affair. It didn't matter what Laban
was trying to do, because God was with Jacob. The
more Laban cheated his son-in-law, the more God
blessed Jacob. God did the thing that Jacob had envi-
sioned. When God gets in the works, things begin
to change.

When someone tells you that it won't work, tell
them that the Lord showed you it would work. When
someone says you can't do it, tell them that the Lord
said you could do it. When someone says that you will
not be able to go, tell them that the Lord said you
would go.

The Devil will tell you that you cannot build the
church of your dreams, but God says you can. Maybe
you can't do it in yourself, but that doesn't matter. God

will do it. When God gets in the arrangements, He will change people's minds and hearts.

When God gets into your real estate deal, He will turn things around and cause the owner to do what he said he would never do.

Men may try to block what you are doing, but they cannot. If God is in it, no man can stop it.

During this difficult period, Laban had changed Jacob's wages ten times. He had tried every way he could to keep Jacob poor so that he could control him, but God blessed Jacob anyway. Men cannot prevent the blessing of God from coming to your life — if you are faithful and cling to His promises.

During the extra six years that Jacob served Laban, his flocks grew so rapidly that they outnumbered those of his father-in-law. He started with nothing, but God took over, and he now had an abundance. He *"increased exceedingly, and had much cattle, and maidservants, and menservants, and camels, and asses."* God knows your circumstances, as well. Trust Him to bless you in the midst of difficulty. Claim all that is rightfully yours, and don't let anyone cheat you out of God's best for your life.

Many believers seem to be sitting back with their arms folded while Satan takes everything that he wants. We must stop him.

When Egypt was about to attack Israel in 1973, Israel was powerless to strike first because of world opinion. So, the Israeli defense forces waited. But after the superior Arab forces struck in a surprise attack on the Jewish religious holiday, Yom Kippur, it took the forces of Israel several days to recover from their pre-liminary losses and to turn the tide of the war. As a result, the military leaders of that nation have sworn that they will never again sit back and allow an enemy to attack them first.

The element of surprise is very important in battle. Gaining initial momentum is very important. Stop sitting back and watching your losses. Go on the offensive; go after what is yours.

Take it all. Israel has possessed only 1/8 of the territory God promised to Moses and Joshua. The rest has never been possessed.

Don't settle for a small portion of your possession in God. Take it all, everything that rightfully belongs to you.

Chapter 12

Don't Be Afraid Of Any Enemy

And the Lord said unto Jacob, Return unto the land of thy fathers, and to thy kindred; and I will be with thee.
I am the God of Bethel, where thou anointedst the pillar, and where thou vowedst a vow unto me: now arise, get thee out from this land, and return unto the land of thy kindred.

Genesis 31:3 & 13

When God spoke to Jacob to return home, He reminded him of Bethel, of his vow, and of the promises

He had made in return. He is faithful to remind us of our obligations to Him. It was time for Jacob to go home.

Remember that commitment. Remember that vow. Remember that promise you made to God. Fortunately, He will not let you forget.

In essence, God is saying to Jacob, "I have done exactly what I said I would do. I have kept you. I have protected you. And, despite the deceitful ways of your uncle, I have blessed you and made you successful. You are now a prosperous man. Now, you must keep your end of the bargain It is time to return to the place of blessing." Men change, but God doesn't change. He is faithful to His promises, no matter how much time passes.

Fortunately, Rachel and Leah were in agreement for once.

> *And Rachel and Leah answered and said unto him, Is there yet any portion or inheritance for us in our father's house? Are we not counted of him strangers? for he hath sold us, and hath quite devoured also our money. For all the riches which God hath taken from our father, that is ours, and our children's: now then, whatsoever God hath said unto thee, do.*   Genesis 31:14-16

These two sisters had been at each other's throat for years. But, now, in this matter, they were in agreement. Their father had treated them badly. He robbed them. He did not keep his promises. He did not fulfill his commitments. They were ready for a move. They were ready for a change. They would take their chances in a strange place. They would travel with their husband to the House of his God, to his land of promise.

So, Jacob with his caravan of family, servants and herds, set out for home.

> *Then Jacob rose up, and set his sons and his wives upon camels; And he carried away all his cattle, and all his goods which he had gotten, the cattle of his getting, which he had gotten in Padanaram, for to go to Isaac his father in the land of Canaan.*
> Genesis 31:17-18

Knowing the duplicity of Laban, the family decided to say nothing to him about their departure. It was hard to tell what he might attempt if he knew. Jacob was afraid that Laban would actually kidnap one of his wives or some of his children in an attempt to prevent him from departing, so nothing was said.

Rachel went quietly to her father's house and took his idols as part of the payment of the debts he owed them. When Laban missed them, he organized a posse to go after Jacob's party. Since Jacob had a head start, it took Laban about a week to overtake him. Laban was very angry that Jacob had left in this way. He was actually thinking about killing him, once he found him. Then, he could take everything Jacob had and return his daughters and their children to his own house. But, one night as he slept along the way, God spoke to him in a dream and warned him to do Jacob no harm.

> *And God came to Laban the Syrian in a dream by night, and said unto him, Take heed that thou speak not to Jacob either good or bad.*
> Genesis 31:24

Laban was not totally obedient. When he caught up to Jacob's party, he accused Jacob of having taken his daughters away at sword point. He said that what hurt him most was not being able to make a great celebration and to have sent his family on its way with *"mirth, and with songs."* "You didn't even let me kiss my daughters good-bye," he lamented. Laban had a way with words. Then he admitted to Jacob that he had intended to do him harm, but that God had warned him not to do it.

> *It is in the power of my hand to do you hurt: but the God of your father spake unto me yesternight, saying, Take thou heed that thou speak not to Jacob either good or bad.*
> Genesis 31:29

Satan is full of bluff. Laban wanted to make sure that Jacob knew he could hurt him if he wanted too. Bluff is what Satan does best. He can only do what God permits him to do, nothing more.

God knows how to deal with our enemies. He knows how to render them helpless and unable to do us harm. The Devil would like to make us believe that he can devour us, but God says to our enemies, "ENOUGH! You can go no further." God knows how to deal with infidels. Don't worry about what they may do.

God knows how to deal with your banker. God knows how to deal with your agent. God knows how to deal with your business partner. God knows how to deal with your mate. Don't worry about what others might do. God has everything under control.

God had a hedge around Job, and He has one around you too. The Enemy will try to make you feel vulnerable, but don't accept his lies. How can you be vulnerable to Satan while God is on your side?

Laban sensed that he was powerless to do Jacob any harm, so the only thing he was concerned about was to recover his valuable idols. He began searching through Jacob's tents for them. He didn't find them because Rachel was sitting on them and declined to get up in her father's presence.

At this point, Jacob sensed his advantage, felt a little righteous indignation, and (not knowing about Rachel's having taken the idols) eloquently pressed his advantage:

> *And Jacob was wroth, and chode with Laban: and Jacob answered and said to Laban, What is my trespass? what is my sin, that thou hast so hotly pursued after me? Whereas thou hast searched all my stuff, what hast thou found of all thy household stuff? set it here before my brethren and thy brethren, that they may judge betwixt us both.*

This twenty years have I been with thee; thy ewes and thy she goats have not cast their young, and the rams of thy flock have I not eaten. That which was torn of beasts I brought not unto thee; I bare the loss of it; of my hand didst thou require it, whether stolen by day, or stolen by night. Thus I was; in the day the drought consumed me, and the frost by night; and my sleep departed from mine eyes. Thus have I been twenty years in thy house; I served thee fourteen years for thy two daughters, and six years for thy cattle: and thou hast changed my wages ten times. Except the God of my father, the God of Abraham, and the fear of Isaac, had been with me, surely thou hadst sent me away now empty. God hath seen mine affliction and the labour of my hands, and rebuked thee yesternight.

Genesis 31:36-42

Laban offered an equally eloquent rebuff to Jacob:

And Laban answered and said unto Jacob, These daughters are my daughters, and these children are my children, and these cattle are my cattle, and all that thou seest is mine: and what can I do this day unto these my daughters, or unto their children which they have born?   Genesis 31:43

But Laban knew that he had lost the battle, and he asked Jacob to enter a pact that they would not try to harm each other in the future, that Jacob would be kind to his daughters and would take no other wives.

A sort of monument was erected as a token of their pledge, a meal was eaten together, prayers were prayed and sacrifices were offered.

A very popular benediction, still used in many churches, was first made between Jacob and Laban and is named for that place: the Mizpah Benediction.

> *The Lord watch between me and thee, when we are absent one from another.* Genesis 31:49

After Laban had kissed his daughters and his grandchildren, he rode quietly away. God can make even our enemies to be at peace with us.

> *That we should be saved from our enemies, and from the hand of all that hate us;* Luke 1:71

> *That he would grant unto us, that we being delivered out of the hand of our enemies might serve him without fear, In holiness and righteousness before him, all the days of our life.*
> Luke 1:74-75

> *When a man's ways please the Lord, he maketh even his enemies to be at peace with him.*
> Proverbs 16:7

No sooner had Laban crossed over the first hill than Jacob had to be concerned about another enemy. He would soon have to confront Esau, his brother. And what would that mean? He had liked the idea of going home, but what awaited him there? When he had left, twenty years before, it was with haste, because Esau was determined to end his life. How would he face his brother now? Remembering Esau's carnality, He decided to offer his brother gifts in exchange for his safety and the safety of his other family members.

> *And Jacob sent messengers before him to Esau his brother unto the land of Seir, the country of Edom. And he commanded them, saying, Thus shall ye speak unto my lord Esau; Thy servant Jacob saith thus, I have sojourned with Laban, and stayed there until now: And I have oxen, and asses, flocks, and menservants, and womenservants: and I have sent to tell my lord, that I may find grace in thy sight.*   Genesis 32:3-5

The message these servants brought back was terrifying to Jacob. Esau was coming to meet him — with four hundred men.

He decided to divide his family and divide his flocks, so that if Esau attacked them in the way, one of the companies could escape, so that not all would be lost. Then, he started doing some serious praying, reminding God again of His promises.

> *And Jacob said, O God of my father Abraham, and God of my father Isaac, the Lord which saidst unto me, Return unto thy country, and to thy kindred, and I will deal well with thee: I am not worthy of the least of all the mercies, and of all the truth, which thou hast shewed unto thy servant; for with*

my staff I passed over this Jordan; and now I am become two bands. Deliver me, I pray thee, from the hand of my brother, from the hand of Esau: for I fear him, lest he will come and smite me, and the mother with the children. And thou saidst, I will surely do thee good, and make thy seed as the sand of the sea, which cannot be numbered for multitude.   Genesis 32:9-12

Still not abandoning his original idea, Jacob separated a gift of animals for his brother and sent them on ahead. It included 200 nanny goats and 20 rams, 200 ewes and 20 rams, 30 female camels with their colts, 40 cows, 10 bulls, 20 female asses with their foals. *If this is the same old Esau,* Jacob was thinking, *when he sees all these animals I am sending him, he will forget everything else and be decent when we finally have to face each other.* But he couldn't be sure of that fact.

Days passed and Jacob could not know what lie ahead. Were they walking into a trap set by Esau? Was he lurking with his men on some hilltop or in some ravine? They didn't know.

They broke their plan when they came to the Jabok Brook and all of them passed over together. And while they were still together, and thus vulnerable, they looked up one day and saw Esau coming with his four hundred men.

And Jacob lifted up his eyes, and looked, and, behold, Esau came, and with him four hundred men.
                    Genesis 33:1

Quickly Jacob divided the group into four, putting each child with its mother. Then, he ranked them in importance to him and placed them accordingly. He put the two handmaidens with their children in the front. Next came Leah and her children. At the very back of the company, and better protected, he put his beloved Rachel and Joseph.

But, in the end, he could not stay back and put any of his wives and children at risk. He decided to go before them all and face Esau first. We can only imagine the tension of the scene as Jacob, with head held high, ready for whatever was coming, strode boldly forward with eyes fixed on his foe.

When he got close enough to see his brother's face, he bowed low before him in a demonstration of humility; he walked a little closer and bowed a second time. He did this seven times, until he was getting very close to Esau. Humility is a powerful tool. It breaks down the most resistant heart. How surprised Jacob must have been when Esau suddenly started running toward him, wildly threw his arms around him, and kissed him!

The scene is described in the Bible with three powerful words:

And they wept.   Genesis 33:4

Esau was eager to meet the members of his brother's family. One by one they were presented to him, and each bowed in his presence. Then Esau began to inquire what Jacob meant by sending such a *"drove"* before him. Jacob frankly told him that it was to find *"grace"* in his eyes.

But Esau had been blessed too. He responded:

> *I have enough, my brother; keep that thou hast unto thyself.* Genesis 33:9

But Jacob insisted:

> *And Jacob said, Nay, I pray thee, if now I have found grace in thy sight, then receive my present at my hand: for therefore I have seen thy face, as though I had seen the face of God, and thou wast pleased with me. Take, I pray thee, my blessing that is brought to thee; because God hath dealt graciously with me, and because I have enough. And he urged him, and he took it.* Genesis 33:10-11

He had left home empty-handed, but now, twenty years later, he was returning full. Isaac had not died when he expected. He was still living. So, Esau's tears had been in vain, for he had lost none of his father's inheritance to Jacob. Now, there was plenty for everyone. Each of them had more than enough.

After they had visited together for a while, Esau suggested that they all travel on together. He offered to lead the way. Jacob had two reasons for declining. One, he said that with his young children and many young animals, he could not keep up a rapid pace and didn't want to hold his brother back. Secondly, he sensed that although he and his brother had made peace and his life was no longer in danger, they were still two very different characters with different goals in life and different motivations.

Esau went his way toward Mt. Seir, and Jacob went another direction, to Succoth, where he built a house and stayed for a while, then to Shechem, where he bought a piece of land and erected an altar to the Lord.

He and his family were safe from their enemies.

Hear me today, it doesn't matter what plans your enemies have for you. If God is with you, you have nothing to fear. David said:

> *Thou preparest a table before me in the presence of mine enemies: thou anointest my head with oil; my cup runneth over.* Psalms 23:5

God blesses us *"in the presence"* of our enemies. They are powerless to stop His blessing. They may try to destroy us, but their plans will not bear fruit. The more they try to harm us, the more God will bless us. Our enemies are inevitably destined for defeat. There can be no other outcome. We have a faithful Shepherd who cares for us unceasingly.

In Bible days, before a shepherd took his flock into a new field, he wandered into the field himself to look around for any snake holes. If he found such a hole, he would pour hog oil around it, keeping the snakes from coming out. When he led his flock into the field, they were safe and could eat, oblivious of any danger. God is looking for some guileless and trusting sheep today.

Our Great Shepherd prepares a table before us; and, whether our Enemy likes it or not, there is nothing he can do about it. We are destined for blessing, despite the enemy's attempts to spoil our victory. None can curse those whom God has blessed.

Jesus said:

> *Blessed are they which are persecuted for righteousness' sake: for theirs is the kingdom of heaven. Blessed are ye, when men shall revile you, and persecute you, and shall say all manner of evil against you falsely, for my sake. Rejoice, and be exceeding glad: for great is your reward in heaven: for so persecuted they the prophets which were before you.* Matthew 5:10-12

Rejoice in the face of the enemy. We are blessed!

Chapter 13

Be Willing to Struggle to Receive All That God Has For You

And Jacob was left alone; and there wrestled a man with him until the breaking of the day. And when he saw that he prevailed not against him, he touched the hollow of his thigh; and the hollow of Jacob's thigh was out of joint, as he wrestled with him.　　　Genesis 32:24-26

As Jacob had crossed over the Jabok and was waiting nervously to see if Esau would appear, he felt restless one evening and decided to get alone for a while. That night he had another encounter with God.

When you get desperate, something happens in your spirit. When you are facing a crisis in life, suddenly your faith comes alive. When you come upon an accident on the side of the road, a supernatural faith and strength go into effect.

Jacob was so distraught with the idea of seeing his brother again that God appeared to him. He wrestled with the Lord until the breaking of the day

Jacob said, "I need You so desperately. If there was ever a time that I needed a word from heaven, it is today. I need it now. If I ever needed the heavens to open for me, I need it now. If I ever needed a miracle, it is now. I will not let you go until you bless me."

When we get serious with God, the answer always comes. When he met Esau the next day, he found his brother with a changed disposition. I don't believe it was changed by the gifts Jacob sent ahead or by his bowing to his brother, although a little humility goes a long way. I believe the attitude of Esau was changed the night before while Jacob wrestled with God.

It is the Lord who puts men down and raises men up.

> *And he changeth the times and the seasons: he removeth kings, and setteth up kings: he giveth wisdom unto the wise, and knowledge to them that know understanding:*   Daniel 2:21

This wrestling with God went on all night long. Finally, toward daybreak, an interesting conversation is recorded.

And he said, Let me go, for the day breaketh.
And he said, I will not let thee go, except thou
bless me.
And he said unto him, What is thy name?
And he said, Jacob.
And he said, Thy name shall be called no more
Jacob, but Israel: for as a prince hast thou power
with God and with men, and hast prevailed.
And Jacob asked him, and said, Tell me, I pray
thee, thy name.
And he said, Wherefore is it that thou dost ask
after my name. And he blessed him there.
                                        Genesis 32:26-29

His name had been Jacob, the deceiver, the sup-
planter. But it would be Jacob no more. God had
changed him. His name would, from that day forth, be
Israel, the prince of God. God knows how to remove the
stigma of the past and put a touch of glory in our souls.

Our government has a program for informers. Those
who enter the program, as star witnesses in key crimi-
nal proceedings, receive a new identity: a new name,
training in a new occupation, and a new place of resi-
dence. Sometimes they even perform plastic surgery
on them to change their appearance. They get all new
legal documents and are set up in business in a new
location. In this way, they can make a new start in life
without fear of the reprisal by those against whom
they are testifying.

When we make a new start in Jesus, we don't need
to go undercover or leave town. We can live our new

life right where we are. We can have a whole new life under our old circumstances; but, praise God, we are new identities entirely. We don't act the same. We don't talk the same. We don't enjoy the same things. We don't want to go to the same places. We are new in God.

The deceit and lies are gone. The cursing and hatred are gone. The defeat and despair are gone; and we are ready to prevail as princes of God. Hallelujah!

Jacob's desperation drove him to pray. It drove him to insist, "I won't let you go until you bless me. I am desperate." It is the desperate, insistent prayer that gets results.

God heard Blind Bartimaeus on the Jericho road. Everyone else told him to be silent and not bother the Master. But his desperate condition would not allow him to be silent. He called, ever more loudly, for the Lord's mercy. And Jesus heard him.

Just because you are in a crisis, don't despair. God let that situation happen for your good. He hasn't left you. He's not dead. Cry out to Him. Don't let go until your blessing comes. I promise you that you will see God's promises fulfilled.

If you claim His promise and stand on it, God cannot fail. But, like Jacob, you must hold on. Don't let go.

Jacob prevailed, but he had to wrestle for a while to show that he was serious about God's help. Don't be surprised if you don't get your answer in a moment. Don't be surprised if you have to get desperate in order to claim your promise. God wants determined and committed people. He has the right to sift and sort us to see who is really serious.

Never fret. You will prevail in the end, if you only hold on.

> *And Jacob called the name of the place Peniel: for I have seen God face to face, and my life is preserved. And as he passed over Penuel the sun rose upon him, and he halted upon his thigh. Therefore the children of Israel eat not of the sinew which shrank, which is upon the hollow of the thigh, unto this day: because he touched the hollow of Jacob's thigh in the sinew that shrank.*
>
> Genesis 32:30-32

God put a permanent mark on Jacob, something that remained with him the rest of his life. You will never be the same after you meet face to face with God. There will be a permanent mark on your life for all to see, a mark of God's glory, the mark of a man or woman who is determined to have God's best and is ready to wrestle to get it.

Chapter 14

Never Resort To Deceit

The wicked worketh a deceitful work: but to him that soweth righteousness shall be a sure reward.
Proverbs 11:18

The thoughts of the righteous are right: but the counsels of the wicked are deceit.
Proverbs 12:5

The wisdom of the prudent is to understand his way: but the folly of fools is deceit.
Proverbs 14:8

There are dozens of powerful passages in the Word of God that teach us the folly of deceit. God is a God of truth and is looking for a people of truth. Deceit is a tool of Satan and a habit of the ungodly.

This is what bothered me so much when, for years, I read the Sunday School lessons concerning Jacob's deceit. The commentators were saying that Jacob's deceit was in the permissive will of God, that God allowed it to happen so that His promises to Jacob could be fulfilled. He could have done it some other way, the writers of the lesson stated, but He allowed it to happen in this way.

That really bothered me. We had too many problems with deception in the ministry as it was. I was convinced that God never needed to use deception, any deception, to achieve His ends. Deception is evil. It is not of God. How could God employ an evil method to do His work?

Jacob lied. There is not other way to say it and no reason to try; and lying never pleases God. He said:

> *Suffer not thy mouth to cause thy flesh to sin;*
> Ecclesiastes 5:6

We must be careful that out mouth does not say one thing while our hands do another. God is never pleased with deceit.

The error of Bible interpretation that led the commentators to say what they did was the idea that what Jacob received by deception was the birthright, which God had shown Rebekah would be Jacob's even before he was born.

One Saturday night, very late, about one o'clock in the morning, I was studying the Sunday School lesson for the next day, and it was about Jacob and Esau. Again, I came upon this abhorrent and contradictory concept, and it troubled me. I asked the Lord to give me some new insight into the reasoning behind the thinking of those who had prepared the lesson.

God spoke to me and showed me that the wrong interpretation was a matter of timing. I jumped up and tried to find a Bible that had a chronology at the top of the page, showing the approximate dates at which specific events occurred. When I finally found one, what the Lord had spoken to my heart was confirmed. Forty years separated the selling of the birthright and Jacob's deception of his father. He bought the birthright when he was thirty-eight, and the deception took place when he was already seventy-eight. They were not, then, one and the same experience. They were two very different matters.

Then, I began to examine what Jacob had gained by his deception and was not surprised to find that he had gained absolutely nothing. Because of what Jacob did, Esau was angry and wanted to kill his brother. Jacob had been forced to flee from home and to live abroad for many years. He left, taking little or nothing in his hands, perhaps only a small lunch to eat along the way. He carried away nothing of his father's goods.

Rebekah, author of the deception, lost the thing she loved the most, and was deprived of the love of her favorite son over the coming years.

When Jacob returned to the land, twenty years later, his father was still alive. Isaac had imagined that he was near death, but he lived on for many years. So, Jacob received nothing of his inheritance until many years later. By that time, he was very rich and didn't even need it.

Isaac lived to be 180 years old; and, when he died, Jacob and Esau had already settled their differences and buried their father together.

> *And Jacob came unto Isaac his father unto Mamre, unto the city of Arbah, which is Hebron, where Abraham and Isaac sojourned. And the days of Isaac were an hundred and fourscore years. And Isaac gave up the Ghost, and died, and was gathered unto his people, being old and full of days: and his sons Esau and Jacob buried him.*
>
> Genesis 35:27-29

Deception gets you nothing. It gets you nowhere. In fact, by using deception, Jacob opened himself up to deception, the deception of Laban and of Leah. How could his father-in-law have deceived him so much? Well, Jacob asked for it by agreeing to utilize deception as a tool himself. How could Leah have been with him all night and he not discover the switch? He had opened himself up to deception, and nothing good can come of deceptive practices. God can't bless them.

Jacob was blessed, not because he deceived his father, but because he met God at Bethel and entered into a personal pact with the God of his fathers.

Jacob was blessed, not because he had tricked his father, but because he believed the promises of God and was not afraid to make a vow to God and to keep that vow, despite the circumstances.

Jacob was blessed, not because he deceived his father, but because he learned to claim what was rightfully his and not to back down when someone tried to take it from him.

Jacob was blessed, not because he deceived his father, but because he was not afraid to face his enemies. He knew that God was on his side.

Jacob was blessed, not because he deceived his father, but because he was not afraid to struggle for what he knew God had for him, holding on until the blessing came.

There is no blessing in deception; and Jacob's deception reaped an evil harvest: personal heartache, a house full of strife, and years of animosity with his Uncle Laban and his brother, Esau.

Jacob lied to his father, and liars will not prosper. If you are somehow benefiting from lies and deceit, it is a false benefit. One day, the plug will be pulled and all your supposed benefits will go quickly down the drain. Just because you are busy does not mean that you are blessed of God. You may seem to have a limited success; but, in the end, your efforts will prove in vain. Some deceitful persons do seem to prosper for a season, but the truth is soon evident.

Many people have ill-gotten wealth, and sometimes we are tempted to envy them. But don't be guilty of this sin. We may not know what goes on behind the high wall of the luxury homes where people have gotten their wealth by unlawful means, but we do know that the curse of sin brings sickness and trouble. Only obedience to God brings happiness and blessings.

Ministers, be careful of the gifts you receive. Sometimes you should refuse gifts — if they are not given in the right spirit or come from unlawful activity. Abraham refused the blessings of the kings of Moab. The prophet Elisha refused the gifts of Naaman. You don't have to depend on man to bless you. God is able. Trust Him. He can take care of His own.

When Jacob led his family and possessions back to the land, he was already one of the wealthiest men of his time, provoking jealousy in those who knew him. But he didn't get any of his wealth by deceit. He got it because the hand of God was upon his life. He got it because he met God under the stars. He got it because he promised God a tithe of everything he earned.

Deception only forced him to leave home empty, while walking with God caused him to return full.

Once you start lying, there is no turning back. One lie leads to another. One deception leads to another. And there is no stopping place. If you start being dishonest, it is difficult to stop. You have to invent another lie to cover the last lie you told.

Many years ago, before I got saved, I saw a card sticking under the glass in a motel room in Newport News, Virginia. It said: **HE WHO TELLS THE TRUTH NEVER HAS TO REMEMBER.** I have never forgotten that little card and its message.

When you don't tell the truth, you have to be always thinking: *Now, how did I tell that story?* And, once you start lying, it is difficult to remember who you lied to last and how the lie went this time. Being truthful is a wonderful release from all that:

> *Let your yea be yea; and your nay, nay; lest ye fall into condemnation.*   James 5:12

Tell it like it is.

Like Jacob, we sometimes want to help God fulfill His promises; but He doesn't need our help. Our deceit won't help Him. Our lie won't help Him. He doesn't need it. He can do what He has promised to do — when we walk in truth.

When Jacob began to lie and cheat, he was lowering himself to the standards of his brother. He became willing to go along with the ideas of his mother to gain financially. He became willing to lower his standards in order to get what he felt belonged to him. But, in the end, all his deceit only brought him heartache and trouble.

God doesn't need your help. Lowering your standards won't bring the promised blessing. It will only limit what God can do for you.

To some people, deception is a fun game. They can imagine themselves helping Jacob: preparing the spiced meat dish, putting those skins on his arms, finding him those clothes with the smell of the field on them, coaching him on how to disguise his voice. But this was no game. This was deadly serious business, and God didn't bless it.

Men are not very hard to deceive, but God is never deceived. You may disguise yourself before men and get away with it, but you cannot disguise yourself before God. He knows who you are and where you are. Jacob, inevitably, had to reap the consequences of his deception.

> *Be not deceived; God is not mocked: for whatsoever*
> *a man soweth, that shall he also reap.*
>   Galatians 6:7

Because Jacob had sown seeds of deceit, he had to reap a harvest. There are some mistakes in life for which we will inevitably pay, even though the blood of Jesus covers a multitude of sins. Jesus is wonderfully forgiving, but there are some fleshly acts and deeds that we simply cannot get away with. The birds will come home to roost. Some of those sins, in fact, will affect other generations.

Do what is right before God, and He will bless you. If we are faithful and honest to do what He has told us, the blessing will be there — without our having to do something dishonest to bring it about.

Why did God permit Jacob to deceive his father? God won't make you do what you don't want to do. He does not force His will upon us. We could just as well ask, Why did He permit Satan to fall from heaven and lose his exalted position as Lucifer, son of the morning? Why did He permit Adam and Eve to fall and lose the perfection of their surroundings and the presence of God with them?

Why? Because He has given us a will to choose right from wrong, to choose to love and serve Him, or not to love and serve Him. It is our choice. He never forces us to obey. He wants to receive our love and obedience, freely given.

Never resort to deceit. Trust God and trust the goodness of His promises, and, without fail, you will prosper.

We need a revival of the fear of God in the church today. Both Isaac and Jacob feared God.

Isaac trembled very exceedingly.   Genesis 27:33

And he was afraid, and said, How dreadful is this place! this is none other but the house of God, and this is the gate of heaven.   Genesis 28:17

Isaac was a man that feared God, and Jacob followed in his footsteps. A healthy fear of God is a wonderful thing, born our of great love. We need much more of it.

We must pray that the fear of God return to the House of God so that God's children will stop playing games with Him and get serious about serving Him. And when we pray this prayer, we may see that God has to strike a few people dead, as He did in the case of Ananias and Sapphira, in Peter's time. If that is what it takes, so be it.

When Esau returned from the fields, and Isaac learned that he had been deceived by Rebekah and

Jacob, he trembled. He was concerned. He was afraid that he had "missed God." It is a fearful thing to hold in your hands the power of blessing and cursing. We can't afford to play around with such power. It can heal, and it can kill.

If God uses you in the gifts of the Spirit, you need to get serious and understand what you are doing. If someone offers you money for the exercise of a spiritual gift, hand their money back to them.

Take Peter's example:

> *And when Simon saw that through laying on of the apostles' hands the Holy Ghost was given, he offered them money, Saying, Give me also this power, that on whomsoever I lay hands, he may receive the Holy Ghost. But Peter said unto him, Thy money perish with thee, because thou hast thought that the gift of God may be purchased with money.* Acts 8:18-20

Jeremiah was thrown into a pit because the king didn't like what he was prophesying. Other prophets were speaking of trouble, but Jeremiah was saying drastic things. Not long after he had the prophet thrown into that pit, however, the king came to ask Jeremiah if he had any word from the Lord.

Jeremiah said that God hadn't changed His mind, that the word was the same as it had been the week before. He wasn't about to play with the treasure of God's Word.

Don't tell people what they want to hear. Don't tell people what will make them feel good. Tell people what God is actually saying.

It is a fearful thing to utter the words, *"thus saith the Lord."* It is better to say nothing at all than to speak in the name of the Lord words that are not His. He warned:

> *I have not sent these prophets, yet they ran: I have not spoken to them, yet they prophesied.*
> Jeremiah 23:21

Isaac's was an awesome responsibility. It made him tremble.

While I was conducting a revival meeting in Florida, a lady came forward with an envelope and asked me to bless it. I started to pray, but was checked by the Spirit. I decided that I had better know what I was blessing, so I took out my glasses and put them on to examine what was in my hand. It turned out to be a lottery ticket. Could I bless what God had cursed? Absolutely not. I prayed for the women, but not for her lottery ticket.

We are great about getting ourselves involved in something, then asking God to bless our ventures. We go about things backwards. Let us first ask God what His will is for us, then we can get involved in something that has His blessing.

Many times, when we ask God to bless our business venture, He has to answer: I never told you to get involved in that. You did it on your own. I can't bless it.

Jacob apparently learned this healthy fear of God from his father. When he got to Bethel and felt that awesome presence of God, he was afraid.

We are going to experience a revival of the fear of God in the Body of Christ.

When Ananias and Sapphira dropped dead at the feet of Peter, the Scriptures say: *"And great fear came on all them that heard these things"* (Acts 5:5). The fear of God, respect for the power and authority of God, brings revival.

Jacob stood in awe at the mighty presence of God. He wasn't afraid that God was going to beat him over the head. He wasn't afraid that God was going to pick up something and kill him. He was overwhelmed with the thought that the Creator of the Universe was present. He was in the House of God. He had entered the Gate of Heaven.

If God is present, we have nothing to worry about.

> *What shall we then say to these things? If God be for us, who can be against us?*   Romans 8:31

When God is on your side, you can be assured that the devil will turn and flee. Don't compromise with the Enemy. Fear God, stand in integrity, and you will always prevail.

Chapter 15

Never Sell Your Birthright

Looking diligently lest any man fail of the grace of God; lest any root of bitterness springing up trouble you, and thereby many be defiled; Lest there be any fornicator, or profane person, as Esau, who for one morsel of meat sold his birthright.
Hebrews 12:15-16

For something so simple and of little, if any, lasting value, Esau sold his birthright. What a profane man! But the truth is that God's people are selling their birthrights every day. Spiritual possessions cannot be bought, but they can be sold. You can't buy a thing from God, but you can sell your inheritance to the Devil, and believers are doing it every day.

By insisting on going through with a one-night stand that you know can only bring heartache for you and others, you sell the power and anointing of God. By insisting on taking a drink with friends or office mates to be accepted by them, you sell the power and anointing of God. By insisting on smoking to "calm your nerves" during a crisis, you sell the power and anointing of God upon your life.

It simply isn't worth it. Cherish and protect the blessing of God in your life. It is priceless. Don't despise your birthright. Hold on to everything that God has promised you. The prize is Jesus and Heaven forever.

A great majority of our Pentecostal people have turned their backs on the heritage we received from our parents and grandparents. God warned the Israelites about this:

> *Thou shalt not remove thy neighbour's landmark, which they of old time have set in thine inheritance, which thou shalt inherit in the land that the Lord thy God giveth thee to possess it.*
>
> Deuteronomy 19:14

> *Cursed be he that removeth his neighbour's landmark. And all the people shall say, Amen.*
>
> Deuteronomy 27:17

Just as Israel had no respect for the ancient landmarks when they entered the land of plenty, our people have cast aside the Faith of Our Fathers, as being old-fashioned, out-of-date, and irrelevant to our times. Nothing could be more wrong!

The old Pentecostal standards for which our fathers paid a high price have been willingly shunted aside in favor of more modern methods. Now we wonder why the church is less a soul-saving station and more an entertainment center

One of the things I deeply appreciate about my own parents is that they refused to compromise through the years. My father was a hardheaded and stubborn man. He didn't care what anybody else said or thought, he was going to do what God told him to do. Now, many years later, I know that his stubbornness was not a negative character trait but a positive one. Someone was always angry with my father, but he wasn't moved by people's anger. The one thing he would not do was compromise. PERIOD!

The church of today has compromised in nearly every regard. We have sold our birthright, our spiritual inheritance, for popularity and acceptance.

In some churches, you will never feel conviction. They specialize in not offending anyone. If you are not offended in some way, you are probably attending the wrong church. God wants us to live under the scrutiny of His heavenly searchlight.

Time is running out. It is too late to play games. Heaven is just over the horizon. One more sunset, and one more sunrise, and we may be there. The Lord is getting us ready. To do that, He has to tell us some hard things, that which He requires of us in order to "make it in." When pastors fail to preach the Word of God and, instead, "tiptoe through the tulips," because they are afraid to step on anyone's toes, (and lose their potential offerings), we are all in trouble.

I attended synagogue one weekend, many years ago, when I was in Dallas, Texas. I was shocked to hear the Rabbi say, "When you know something is wrong, and you keep silent, it is a sin."

He was right. We often sin in fear of offending. We often sin in fear of alienating people. We often sin in fear of being branded extremists.

But young people especially are tired of hearing the same platitudes every Sunday. They have tried the world and are ready for a real experience in God. They thought they could find peace and joy in getting high, but drugs only brought them sickness and death. They tried promiscuous sex, but it only brought them disappointment and venereal disease. Alcohol left them hung over and depressed. They are ready for something real and lasting.

Esau sold his glory for momentary pleasure. Don't repeat his tragic mistake.

The greatest lesson we learn from the epic lives of the two brothers, Jacob and Esau, is that birthright and blessing go hand in hand. If you sell your birthright, you will eventually lose your blessing. Although they are different, one follows the other. Jacob didn't have to cheat to get the blessing. The blessing was destined for him from the beginning because he had chosen God's part.

Don't let the devil trick you into compromise. He will always declare that he has something better; but he has always been a liar. Don't give up what God has given you for anything this world has to offer. Your spiritual heritage is priceless. And there is nothing to match it, or even come close to it, in this world.

All the money in the world can't buy spiritual blessings. If are dying from cancer, a million dollars can't buy your healing. You cannot buy faith.

Some people think, "When I get a little money in the bank, then I'll find time for God"; but those people never seem to find time for God; and, consequently, they will never be as successful as God intended them to be.

Somebody asked a millionaire, "How much more money would it take to make you happy?" Not surprisingly, his answer was, "Just a little more." Money never satisfies. No amount of money ever satisfies. Only Jesus satisfies. Some people who live in a shack on the side of a road are the happiest people you will ever meet. The secret is that they have Jesus.

David knew the value of the blessing of God. He said:

I had rather be a doorkeeper in the house of my God, than to dwell in the tents of wickedness.
                                                                     Psalms 84:10

Esau couldn't see that because he had no spiritual eyesight. He put a value of ZERO on his spiritual heritage. That's how blind he was. We must, first, recognize the value of what we have, and, secondly, protect it. Jesus said, in the Revelation to John:

> *Behold, I come quickly: hold that fast which thou hast, that no man take thy crown.*
>
> Revelation 3:11

Treasure the gift of tongues; treasure prophecy; treasure the gifts of healing; treasure the call of God upon your life. No amount of money can purchase these great gifts. Treasure the anointing.

Paul encouraged Timothy to remember his spiritual heritage:

> *When I call to remembrance the unfeigned faith that is in thee, which dwelt first in thy grandmother Lois, and thy mother Eunice; and I am persuaded that in thee also.*   2 Timothy 1:5

Two men can look at the same item and value it in a different way. To one person, the item may seem to be worth only $5. The other person may know more about the item, however, and may know that it is actually worth several hundred dollars. It is a matter of understanding the true value.

Jacob knew the value of the birthright. He wanted it. There is nothing wrong with that. He had been biding his time, looking for an opportunity that he was sure would come. He could tell, by the way Esau was living, that he did not value greatly his birthright. He was sure that his day would come, and it did.

I have often gone to auctions and bought very valuable equipment for the camp for a few dollars. I got it so cheap because nobody was present who valued that equipment.

A diamond before it is cleaned and cut and polished doesn't look like much. Most of us, if we saw one, might not put much value on it. When it is cut and polished, it is so beautiful and so valuable that we would all like to have one.

We always make a mistake when we seek material things first. The result is that we lose out even on the material things. We must always seek God and His blessing first.

In our present world, money is a great motivator. Fame is a great motivator. Prestige is a great motivator. If we could seek after God in the same measure that the people of the world seek money, or pleasure, or advancement, we would have so much more than we actually do.

It is not wrong for us to have things, but we must learn to hold all this world's goods very lightly. When we do, God lets us keep them longer. If we hold things too tightly, God knows they are dangerous to our soul, and He might have to take them from us to keep us close to Him.

When we love Him above all else, there is no limit to His blessing. He said:

And every one that hath forsaken houses, or brethren, or sisters, or father, or mother, or wife, or

children, or lands, for my name's sake, shall receive
an hundredfold, and shall inherit everlasting life.
                                                    Matthew 19:29

He is ready to give us 100 times more than we can give up for His name's sake. Prosperity is no problem with God. What we must do is to keep our souls well. That means some prayer and fasting. What a privilege! Every time I have sought God in fasting and prayer, financial blessings have come to me. I have never fasted for a certain amount of money. It just comes as a result of my spiritually seeking God. When we spend all our time preoccupied with the financial aspect of life, we lose so many of the blessings God wants to give us. Concentrate on the spiritual.

Job lost everything, but his spirit remained right before God. We consider the life of Job to have been a great tragedy because he lost everything, but the truth is that he only lost physical things. He maintained his integrity before God.

How can we be so concerned about losing a job, so concerned about losing our health, so concerned about losing a right, and so unconcerned about losing our spirituality?

If Job's spirit had gone bad, he never would have recovered. But because his spirit remained correct before God, God was obligated to bless him with more than he had ever had.

God was so pleased with Solomon's attitude. He didn't ask for riches. He didn't ask for his enemies. He asked for a right heart and for wisdom. And God gave him that — plus everything else he hadn't asked for — until he was the envy of the kings of the earth.

We can have the birthright, and we can have the blessings, as well. We are kings and priests unto God. We can have them — if we can get our values changed. Many of us are praying selfish prayers. If we are asking for a new house only to feel proud of what we have, we are in error. If we plan to start a prayer meeting and use that house for the glory of God, that pleases Him. If we ask for a new car only because we like the newer model, that won't work. If we want a new car to travel for God and to bring other people to church, He will answer that prayer. If you want money for the right reasons, that's okay. If you need anything to use for a proper reason, God hears your cry.

Jesus showed us the value of the soul and the treasures of the spiritual life:

> *For whosoever will save his life shall lose it; but whosoever shall lose his life for my sake and the gospel's, the same shall save it. For what shall it profit a man, if he shall gain the whole world, and lose his own soul? Or what shall a man give in exchange for his soul?* Mark 8:35-37

> *Lay not up for yourselves treasures upon earth, where moth and rust doth corrupt, and where thieves break through and steal: But lay up for yourselves treasures in heaven, where neither moth nor rust doth corrupt, and where thieves do*

not break through nor steal: For where your treasure is, there will your heart be also.

Matthew 6:19-21

It is up to each of us to develop a value system. Yours may be based on worldly concepts, or it can be based on the eternal Word of God. It is your choice. I have made my choice. The blessings of God are the most important thing in my life. If the stock market fails and the governments of the world fall and our currency loses all its value, I will have nothing to fear. My faith is in God who made heaven and earth.

I will not sell that — for any price.